$16.95

D1046686

THE EMERGING PARISH

THE EMERGING PARISH

The Notre Dame Study of Catholic Life Since Vatican II

Jim Castelli and
Joseph Gremillion

1817

Harper & Row, Publishers, San Francisco

Cambridge, Hagerstown, New York, Philadelphia, Washington
London, Mexico City, São Paulo, Singapore, Sydney

THE EMERGING PARISH: *The Notre Dame Study of Catholic Life Since Vatican II.* Copyright © 1987 by James J. Castelli and Joseph Gremillion. All rights reserved. Printed in the United States of America. No part of this book may be used or reproduced in any manner whatsoever without written permission except in the case of brief quotations embodied in critical articles and reviews. For information address Harper & Row, Publishers, Inc., 10 East 53rd Street, New York, NY 10022. Published simultaneously in Canada by Fitzhenry & Whiteside, Limited, Toronto.

FIRST EDITION

Library of Congress Cataloging-in-Publication Data

Gremillion, Joseph.
  The emerging parish.

  Bibliography: p.
  Includes index.
  1. Parishes—United States—History—20th century.
2. Catholic Church—United States—History—20th
century. I. Castelli, Jim. II. Title.
BX1746.G64 1987 282'.73 87–45168
ISBN 0-06-061323-8

87 88 89 90 91 RRD 10 9 8 7 6 5 4 3 2 1

Contents

LIST OF TABLES

Foreword

The Notre Dame Study of Catholic Parish Life, which this book reports, is a service of research, analysis, and interpretation provided by Notre Dame University to the Catholic people of our country, concerning their church at the level of local community. I know that many leaders and members of other Christian churches, and of other faiths, will also be interested in these findings, as well as scholars and writers concerned with American society, its values, institutions, and movements.

This book sets forth in orderly manner the very significant effects of Vatican Council II (1962–65) upon American Catholics, as a whole and in their local communities—in towns and villages, inner cities and suburbs, among all ages and ethnic groups. This it does within the wider historical context of Catholics moving as a body since the 1940s into the mainstream of American life and leadership, following the admirable struggles of immigrant forebears toward economic sufficiency, political participation, and social status.

Integral to the education and growth of students in our Catholic university is the call to participate generously after graduation in the life and leadership of their parish and community. This is our ongoing gift to the local church nationwide. Through this study, we convey Notre Dame's admiration for and gratitude to the pastors, staffs, and lay leaders of the 19,500 parishes which comprise the 185 dioceses of the Catholic church, USA, serving regularly over 52 million faithful. We particularly thank the thousands of parishioners and staff who have cooperated with Notre Dame in making the study.

The changes wrought within parishes since Vatican II, especially increased activity by parishioners, a main focus of the study, are of deep interest as well to universities such as Notre Dame. On our campus we also perceive broader Christian commitment among our students, through more vital liturgies and leadership, with stronger sense of community, for ecumenical and social concern. We welcome and foster this new surge of religious awareness, nourished by the fresh theological and spiritual fonts of the Council. We expect our alumni, present and future, to participate more fully in the post-Vatican II church of America, now taking mature shape in the emerging parishes throughout the land.

Two Notre Dame bodies are collaborating in this study: the Institute for Pastoral and Social Ministry and the Center for the Study of Contemporary Society. The director of the latter for ten years, Dr. David C. Leege, has headed the scientific team and has written most of the published reports which provide the basis for this book. Three diocesan priests—Msgr. John Egan, Father Philip Murnion, and Msgr. Joseph Gremillion—have brought to the project their accumulated pastoral experience totaling over a hundred years. Egan was founding director of Notre Dame's Institute for Pastoral and Social Ministry, and Gremillion was his successor. Murnion was former executive for the parish project of the National Conference of Catholic Bishops, and now heads the National Pastoral Life Center.

To them and their two-score collaborators in this cooperative endeavor of scholarly research and pastoral insight, I voice warm gratitude. Deep appreciation is also expressed to the Lilly Endowment, Inc., which provided the funding for this pioneering probe into the role of religion in our time among the American people, in and through the local Catholic community—the parish emerging since Vatican II.

The Reverend Theodore M. Hesburgh, C.S.C.
President
University of Notre Dame
April, 1987

1. The Emerging Parish

Jesus Christ calls out, "Come, follow me," and men and women respond; that is how the Church began and how it continues today here in America. But, staying only overnight, a couple of days, a week or so in successive towns and villages, Christ did not establish local communities of his followers before his death. Fifty days after the first Easter, the first local congregation of the Church gathered in Jerusalem on Pentecost Sunday in the year 30.

Today, 1,950 years later, there are 1,800,000 local Christian congregations throughout the world with some 1,550,000,000 adherents. More than 200,000,000 Christians live in the United States, where they form more than 385,000 local congregations.

There are 210,000 Catholic parishes worldwide, plus 158,000 additional congregations—mission stations and chapels lacking formal parochial status, served from neighboring parishes—for a total of 368,000 "pastoral centers" serving a total of 825,000,000 Catholics.

There are 19,313 Catholic parishes in the United States in 185 dioceses (called "particular churches"). These parishes are established according to the Code of Canon Law, Canon 515, which defines a parish as "a definite community of the Christian faithful established on a stable basis within a particular church; the pastoral care of the parish is entrusted to a pastor as its own shepherd under the authority of the diocesan bishop. . . . A legitimately erected parish has juridic personality by the law itself."

But this "juridic personality" conveys little of the human personality of a parish—the communion and the concern, the caring and tension, the yearning, seeking, and mystery. The parish is a living entity.

And that entity has been reshaped by a dramatic event in the history of the Catholic church—the Second Vatican Council

(1962–65). While Vatican II did not focus on the parish per se, it set in motion substantial reform and updating within Catholic parishes throughout the world and particularly in the United States. The Council focused on the broad questions of the nature, life, and ministry of the church, on ecclesial relations among Christian bodies and with other faiths, and on the role of the church in today's world.

Its two principal documents, the *Dogmatic Constitution on the Church (Lumen Gentium)*, and the *Pastoral Constitution on the Church in the Modern World (Gaudium et Spes)*, provide theological foundations and pastoral principles which have brought significant and continuing changes in the Catholic church at all levels—global, regional, and national, especially among dioceses and within parish communities. Ten additional documents of Vatican II exercise direct impact on the updating of parish life: those on liturgy, laity, bishops, priests, religious life, priestly formation, education, communications, missions, and ecumenism. One major fruit of the Council was opening the church to continued reflection, critique, and experiment.

Out of all these documents emerged several themes which have affected the whole church and the individual parish as well—the famous opening of a window into the world; the conception of the church not as an institution but as the People of God; and shared participation in the life of the church. These themes of leadership, laity, and community echo throughout life in the emerging parish of the United States in the 1980s.

The title image of "the emerging parish" reflects movement sparked by the overall impact of Vatican II upon the Catholic church—at global, national, diocesan, and neighborhood levels. More than fifty million American Catholics now experience themselves as today's People of God, primarily through the life, liturgy, witness, ministry, and community of a particular parish. "Emerging" also connotes a journey still in progress along the path pointed to by Vatican II. While we cannot say what the "final" post-Vatican II parish will look like, plenty of signposts point toward the future.

Where have the twenty years of Vatican II reform taken the American Catholic parish? Is it a place where people find God, where they join together in meaningful worship and prayer, where they satisfy their yearning to know God and serve their neighbors? What is the quality of leaderhip and the nature of participation? What ministries do parishes perform well and where do they come up short of peoples' needs and God's expectations? What directions already emerge to reshape parish life of the 1990s and the year 2000?

Those are some of the questions which prompted the Notre Dame Study of Catholic Parish Life, an unparalleled and unprecedented multidisciplinary study of Catholic parishes in the United States. The study has produced some fascinating, and often startling, answers.

David Leege observed that "if a major purpose of Vatican II was to reinstate the sense that all Christians—lay, priests and religious—are responsible for corporate life in the local parish, then Vatican II is succeeding in the United States. The American Church is participatory not only in religious ritual but especially in shared responsibility for ministry. Even in ritual, people have noticed how much more active and expressive they are expected to be. Parish policy-making and governing patterns are not yet clearly demarcated, but the effort to find parish governance mechanisms as effective or more effective than parish councils continues. The picture of a parish where Father O'Brien took care of God, Sister Cerita ran the school and the people met their Mass obligations and said 'Hail Marys' would be a woefully inadequate stereotype of U.S. Catholic parishes in the 1980s, if ever."

Consider these findings:

- Beyond the pastor, 83 percent of those identified as the leadership within Catholic parishes, paid or unpaid, are laypersons. Even among the paid staff with responsibilities for key programs, 57 percent are lay. Among the unpaid leadership responsible for central parish activities, 94 percent are lay.
- In 64 percent of the parishes, leadership involves a combination

of pastor, religious, and laity. The emerging ministerial teams of the 1980s are overwhelmingly lay. In fact, in an estimated 10 percent of the parishes, it is fair to say that nonpriests—a married deacon or a group of laypersons—are the central figures.

- Half of all parish-connected Catholics (48 percent) take part in some parish activity outside of Mass. This reflects the growth since Vatican II of new parish programs such as adult education.
- Core Catholics, those who are active parish members, practice the same kind of "pick and choose" Catholicism found among inactive Catholics; they follow church teaching when they agree with it and reject it when they do not.
- American Catholics have adopted the rhetoric and vision of Vatican II which views the church as the People of God, and in many parishes, though certainly not all, the ideal of parish community has become a reality.
- American Catholics have internalized Vatican II reforms and want even more in the way of reforms and new services and programs from their parishes.
- One heritage of the Council is a "liturgical smorgasbord" in which parishes provide different style liturgies for different segments of the parish community.
- American parishes are far more varied in size, style, and vitality than most Catholics recognize.

THE NOTRE DAME STUDY

There is little question that social research on the Catholic church is a growth industry in the United States. American Catholics have never had a strong in-house research tradition. Many Protestant bodies established offices for research and planning early in this century. These churches were mainly American-based. American businesses, government, and universities had long traditions of research, and American Protestant churches operated within that research and planning environment.

American Catholics, however, were a minority denomination in the United States and part of a church with headquarters in the

Vatican, not in the United States. The Vatican's research and planning efforts derived from theological and scholarly traditions very different from empirical social inquiry. The Catholic church within the United States was internationally centralized, but nationally decentralized—its dioceses reported not to a national office, but to the Vatican. The National Conference of Catholic Bishops became a major institution in the church only recently, and it wasn't until the 1980s that the media began taking the bishops' pastoral letters seriously. Finally, the national offices that deal with research within the Catholic church are skeletal, outside of Catholic education, and only about one-fourth of the dioceses have research staffs, which still must struggle to win appreciation for their contribution to the church's ministries.

Into that official vacuum, however, stepped a number of social scientists and pollsters. Important small-scale studies pioneered by Jesuit Father Joseph Fichter in the 1940s were followed by large-scale national surveys initiated by Father Andrew Greeley at the National Opinion Research Center at the University of Chicago in the 1960s and 1970s. Other major national polls have kept track of Catholic opinion.

Neither church nor public now lacks information about the attitudes and behaviors of American Catholics, particularly regarding controversial issues on which a sizeable proportion of Catholics have taken positions at odds with church teaching. Much of the public discussion, however, did not separate out Catholics by their degree of church involvement, lumping those who never attend Mass with those who attend several times a week.

Further, the public discussion treated American Catholics as an amorphous group, yet none of us exist in the aggregate. We typically learn and live our religious values in a family, and that family's values are in turn shaped by and help to shape the religious practices of a local parish. One of the founders of modern sociology, Emile Durkheim, argued that smaller communities—families, churches, etc.—develop their own "moral consensus" and that much of what we tell about the past, interpret in the present, or hope for in the future is instilled in these communities. The contemporary sociologist Robert Bellah points to parishes as "communities of memory" that nurture our identification with larger community purposes and standards well beyond the utilitarian demands of American individualism.

Most previous research surveyed beliefs, attitudes, and practices of individual members; in a few studies, the structure of a single parish or a handful of parishes was examined. But no study had ever systematically examined both individuals and parish structures in the context of liturgical practices and historical developments across a broad variety of parishes.

The need for an overall study of Catholic parish life in the 1980s received strong encouragement from the United States bishops' 1980 statement, *The Parish: A People, A Mission, A Structure* and from programs and publications which followed that statement. The Notre Dame Study of Catholic Parish Life was launched with the idea of combining analysis of parish structure, leadership, and performance with study of parishioners' views and behavior. This approach made the study unique. A second notable factor was the interdisciplinary character of the research. It involved sociology, history, liturgy, doctrine, and spirituality, together with an analysis of organizational structure and decision making as a community, and a survey of parishioners' beliefs, practices, and communal faith experiences.

Phase I of the study began in 1982. Questionnaires were sent to 1,850 parishes, 10 percent of those in existence at the time. Usable responses were received from 1,099 pastors or administrators for a 59 percent return rate, by far exceeding the usual level of voluntary cooperation for mail questionnaires.

A third significant feature was the study's in-depth focus in Phase II on 36 parishes chosen as representative from the 1,099 parish responses. Based on these reports, the nation was divided into six geographical regions: northeast, south Atlantic, south central, Midwest, intermountain, and Pacific. Within each region, parishes were chosen as representative on the basis of size, geography, organizational complexity, dynamism of activities, leadership and participation, and ethnic background.

Phase II involved the following research:

• Questionnaires were distributed to those on the membership lists of the thirty-six representative parishes as well as to pastors, staff members, and volunteers. The study sent questionnaires to 4,555 scientifically selected parishioners and received responses from 59 percent, or 2,667 individuals. Questionnaires were also sent to 117 paid staff members with a 76 percent response rate and to 262 volunteers with a 77 percent return rate. The fact that it took several hours to fill out the questionnaires suggests that respondents were highly motivated. At the same time, however, 13 percent of those responding said they attended Mass only several times a year or less.

All in all, study researchers say that it is reasonable to believe that the parishioner sample is a representative sample of American Catholics with ties to parishes. How large a group is that? Gallup surveys indicate that 28 percent of Americans identify themselves as Catholics, which amounts to some 67 million people. Gallup figures also show that 80 percent of American Catholics claim to be church members. Applying this 80 percent, we get a figure very close to the 52 million Catholics reported in the *Official Catholic Directory,* which bases its figures on reports from dioceses which, in turn, base their figures on reports from parishes. We believe it is reasonable, then, to suggest that the *Official Catholic Directory* figure of 52 million people is a good rough estimate of the number of parish-connected Catholics in the United States.

• Two-person teams, composed of a liturgist and a social scientist, were sent to each parish for on-site visits, including a weekend. These sixteen researchers were brought to Notre Dame for training sessions. They received three research "instruments" to use in their visits: one to describe changes in the floor plan and physical layout of the church since 1964 when Vatican II issued its new constitution on the liturgy; another to record observations of two regular Saturday evening and Sunday Masses; and a third to interview decision-makers regarding liturgical planning, sacramental preparation, and degree of guidance from diocesan or other local sources.

• The on-site researchers also developed ethnographic and historical reports by studying parish histories and publications and interviewing pastors and parish leaders to prepare accounts of parish influence structures, the parish's own sense of community, the parish's place in the life of the local community, and its most notable positive and negative features.

• Six historians prepared histories of the six regions within the United States church. Jay Dolan, who supervised the overall historical part of the study, states, "Previous studies of the Catholic parish had neglected history and thus had unwittingly contributed to the historical amnesia so prevalent in American society. . . . Catholics will never understand who they are as American Catholics unless they first know who they were. . . . For anyone desirous of comprehending the history of the American Catholic people, a study of the parish is essential. It was the hinge on which their religous world turned."

Vatican II has already awakened Core Catholics from the sleepy myth of an unchanging church. The following pages profile the dramatic dilemma of a rock-founded church moving amidst the fast-flowing currents of American culture and society.

NOTE

This chapter is based on Report 1 by David Leege and Joseph Gremillion.

2. A Regional History of American Parish Life

The Catholic church in the United States, mused Archbishop John Hughes of New York in the mid-nineteenth century, is unique because, here, the people came first, and the church followed. If he were speaking in the post-Vatican II language of today, of course, he would say that the church in the form of the People of God came first, and the church in its institutional form followed. But the fact Archbishop Hughes pointed out, however expressed, has shaped the history of Catholic people and Catholic parishes in the New World. In Europe, the church, it seemed, was always there. In Latin America, the church sent missionaries to convert the native populations. But in the United States, Catholics came from Europe of their own accord, seeking new life and new opportunities. From Europe to northeastern towns and midwestern farms, moving west frontier after frontier, crowding into cities by the late 1800s and then into suburbs by the 1950s, Catholic lay people have been pioneers. And the church has followed, to serve and, in a sense, to reclaim its own.

Throughout its time in the New World, the American Catholic laity has maintained a leadership spirit within the parish and the church community. That spirit has been overshadowed by other forces at various times in the history of the United States parish, but it has never disappeared. Since Vatican II, that leadership spirit has been reenergized by a combination of domestic social momentum among American Catholics themselves and the theological and spiritual rationale of the Council.

In this chapter, we will sketch out a brief history of the American parish to set a context in which to understand the findings of the Notre Dame study. This is not a history of the American

Catholic church as an institution or of American Catholics themselves but a history of the American Catholic parish and the role
it has played in the life of the church.

"There is always something fascinating about the history of a
Catholic parish," the late Archbishop Joseph Rummel of New Orleans wrote in 1948. "Usually modest and humble in its begin-
nings, it grows larger, more dignified and more efficient with the
years. It is almost human in its development, and quite under-
standingly so, for it is composed of vibrant human beings and is
intimately influenced by their genius, their moods and their fortunes. Equally true is it that a parish reflects the conditions, civic,
social, economic, as well as religious, that prevail at various stages
of its existence and development."

In addition to the impact of local conditions and personalities,
the life of a parish is also shaped by broad social movements which
are not always easily understood at the time—for example, the
impact of urbanization in the late nineteenth and early twentith
centuries and the impact of suburbanization in the recent decades.
At the same time, parish life feels the impact of decisions made
by church leaders at the Vatican and in Washington.

AN IMMIGRANT CHURCH

The dominant fact in the life of the American parish is the fact
that, in the United States, Catholicism began as an immigrant
religion in a nation with an overwhelmingly Protestant culture.
In 1790, Catholicism was a small sect of some 90,000 people with
considerably less influence than Quakers, Unitarians, or Deists.
By 1815, the number of Catholics had more than doubled to
200,000. But by the middle of the nineteenth century, a potato
famine in Ireland and poverty and upheaval in Germany had pro-
pelled large numbers of Catholics to the American shores. By
1850, the Roman Catholic Church, with 1,334,500 members, had
become the largest religious denomination in the new "Protestant"
country. By 1860, the number of Catholics had surged to more
than 3,000,000. As immigrants, Catholics were laborers and set

the tone for a working-class church—Catholics worked in factories in the northeast, spread throughout the country building canals and railroads, and went west with other settlers seeking to find their fortunes in the mines. Catholics were also farmers, as hungry for land and as hardworking as any other Americans who pushed the frontier westward.

This rapid growth set the stage for several themes which were to dominate the church for a century. The history of Catholic parishes often seems a history of fund raisers and new buildings, and for a time it was common to joke about the church's "edifice complex." But it was the Catholic people who demanded the buildings for churches, schools, and meeting halls to provide the symbols and instruments of a worship community. Buildings and, therefore, finances posed a problem for the church in both urban and rural areas.

In the early days of the nation, Catholics were literally few and far between. To most observers of American church history, the Methodists stand out as the denomination of "circuit riders," ministers on horseback who rode the frontier bringing the faith to settlers. But the early Catholic priests were also circuit riders, covering vast stretches of territory where the only churches were the home of families who strove to keep their faith alive without benefit of chapel, clergy, or congregation.

Traveling priests worked to link these families into "stations" (groups of families) and later "missions" (congregations and chapels without a resident priest) which eventually achieved parish status with the assignment of a permanent pastor. Lay people led these small religious communities in the long periods of time when no priests were available. Many of the first priests were immigrants themselves. The first priests in the south Atlantic region were French, German, and Irish. All Hallows College in Ireland provided almost half of the priests in California between 1850 and 1880.

In urban areas, the church struggled to keep up with the constant overcrowding caused by the waves of new immigrants flowing into the cities. The church's inability to provide priests and church buildings in sparsely populated areas was responsible for the fact that many Catholics—"strayed sheep"—joined more accessbile Protestant churches.

The fact that the laity came before the clergy in most parts of the country determined the form of governance that characterized the American Catholic parish until the mid-nineteenth century. It was common for lay leaders to hold a congregation together until a priest was appointed. When a priest was appointed, he had to learn to work with the lay leaders. Parishes adopted a system common in American Protestant churches and in some European countries—the laity elected lay trustees to work with the priest in managing the affairs of the parish.

Lay trustees collected money, paid the bills, provided the priest's salary, and took care of legal affairs. But by the early 1800s, some trustees also tried to hire and fire priests. This created conflict, not only with parish priests, but with bishops who, according to church law, retained sole authority to hire and fire priests. Bishops eventually solved the problem by seeing that every new church opened was vested in the bishops' name. The last "vestry"—another name for lay trustees—died off by 1900 in the southeast, where priests were still scarce.

The lay trustee system was used extensively in the Northeast. In the Midwest, it was highly popular with German Catholics, less so with the Irish. In fact, the lay trustee system appeared in virtually every section of the country before it was ended by bishops who wanted to consolidate power and did so under the concept of "corporation sole" in which the bishop owned all property in a diocese.

Jay Dolan says, "History has not been kind to this tradition in American Catholicism and has wrongly depicted the trustee system and lay trustees as detrimental to Catholic life. Though the problem certainly had some flaws because of irascible laymen and authoritarian priests, it worked remarkably well in numerous parish communities where, in the words of Bishop John England of Charleston, South Carolina, 'The laity are empowered to cooperate, but not to dominate.' In a sense, the post-Vatican II American parish is now returning to its lay roots."

The fact that Catholicism was an immigrant church was responsible for another development crucial to the life of the parish. The influx of Catholic immigrants triggered a negative reaction among many white Anglo-Saxon Protestants, who felt threatened by change and greeted the newcomers with bigotry and occasional violence. The Know-Nothing political movement of the 1840s and 1850s was based on anti-Catholicism. In 1854, the party elected seventy-five members to Congress, in addition to local government posts. There were other incidents of anti-Catholicism:

• In 1854, native inhabitants battled immigrant Irish in St. Louis, and the Catholic church in Helena, Arkansas, was burned down. In 1855, hostile nativists attacked immigrants on election day, August 6, in Louisville; twenty-two people were killed and many more were injured.

• In the 1850s, the Vigilance Committee targetted Irish Catholics in San Francisco and Mexican Catholics in the mining towns. In 1855, a Catholic church was burned down in Drytown, California.

• Catholic churches were burned down in Norfolk, Virginia, in 1856 and in Portsmouth, Virginia, in 1858; Know-Nothing supporters were suspected in both cases.

• In the Southeast after 1910, anti-Catholicism was fostered by those such as populist leader Tom Watson, whose *Watson's Jeffersonian Magazine* published articles with titles such as "The Roman Catholic Hierarchy: Deadliest Menace to Our Liberties and Our Civilization."

• In 1914, a Catholic church in Birmingham and a school in Pratt, Alabama, were burned down. Two years later, armed guards at Birmingham's Catholic churches drove off attackers. In the 1920s, Catholics in Arkansas and Alabama were subject to convent search laws. In 1921, Father James Coyle, pastor of Saint Paul's Church in Birmingham, was murdered in front of a witness on his front porch by a Methodist minister. The minister, Edwin

Stephenson, was outraged because Coyle had officiated at a marriage between Stephenson's daughter and a Catholic. Stephenson, defended by future Supreme Court Justice Hugo Black, was found not guilty by reason of insanity. (Ironically, by 1980, thirty-five percent of Catholic marriages in the south central region included a Protestant partner; in more than half of the region's dioceses, there were more Catholic-Protestant than Catholic-Catholic marriages.)

• Anti-Catholicism reached its peak on the West Coast in the 1920s in Oregon when the Ku Klux Klan had enough strength to push through a state law requiring every student to attend a public school. The act would have forced Oregon Catholic schools out of existence. In 1925, the United States Supreme Court, in *Pierce v. Society of Sisters,* ruled the law unconstitutional.

The nativism that greeted Catholic immigrants intensified the natural desire of an immigrant group to stick together. Catholics looked to the parish as both a haven from prejudice and a means of becoming socialized into their new home, of becoming "Americanized." In addition to serving as a kind of sanctuary, Catholic parishes echoed another social development of the time—the "total parish" reflected the spread of "Utopian communities" in the northeast and elsewhere in the 1850s.

While nativism was a major problem for Catholics and their parishes, it was not the only pattern of Protestant-Catholic relations. Charles Nolan reports that in the south central region "Protestants often offered the hospitality of their churches to visiting Catholic priests and donated land and/or money to help their Catholic neighbors build a church. . . . Protestants also contributed to the establishment of the first Catholic churches in Mobile, Nashville, and Memphis. Non-Catholics joined their Catholic neighbors in rebuilding the Catholic church in Selma, Alabama, after its destruction during the [Civil] War." As the parish bazaar emerged as a major form of fund raising, particularly in California, it attracted support from non-Catholics as well as parishioners. In the Southeast, particularly in Florida, Catholic schools were frequently supported and patronized by Protestants in the early part of the twentieth century.

CONSOLIDATION

By 1880, the basic parish structure of the Northeast and Midwest, home for about 70 percent of American Catholics, was in place. Most Catholics were Irish and German, and because the Irish had the advantage of already speaking English, they moved much more quickly into the mainstream of American life—and into the leadership of the church, which soon became known as "the Irish church."

But in the second half of the nineteenth century, the Irish and Germans were joined by Catholics from a broad array of European backgrounds—Italians, Poles, eastern Europeans. The church in the Northeast and Midwest responded by establishing "national parishes"—parishes devoted to members of a specific ethnic group and usually served by a priest from that ethnic group. These national parishes in particular served as a means of socializing new Americans. In 1880, 8 percent of the parishes in the Northeast were national parishes. This rose to 17 percent in 1900 and 21 percent by 1930. In Manhattan, 50 percent of the parishes opened between 1902 and 1918 were national, one-third of them Italian.

Interestingly enough, bishops on the West Coast, who had fewer Catholics to deal with but still served an immigrant population, were reluctant to establish national parishes. Instead, they worked with immigrants within geographic parish boundaries, employing a priest who spoke the group's language. Today's Catholic parishes, in serving new Hispanic and Asian immigrants, are much closer to the model used by the West Coast bishops in the nineteenth century, encouraging ethnic communities to exist within and integrate with the territorial parish. Perhaps one reason for this is the unstated assumption that, while the national parishes served many purposes, they also created a certain amount of insularity from the rest of the church and the rest of the society.

As the church became more institutionalized in the last half of the nineteenth century, patterns of leadership changed. Dolan says, "As the numbers of clergy increased and the institutionalized church became better organized with the establishment of numerous dioceses, bishops and pastors assumed control of the local Church, and the laity were left to 'pay, pray, and obey,' as one pundit put it."

Joseph Casino writes that "at the head of this whole parish apparatus was the parish priest. Initially, he was seen, by himself and by his parishioners, as a laborer among the poor and sick, often wasting himself in tireless service to his people. By the 1850s, however, the image of the priest had changed. His clerical leadership became measured in terms of the number of buildings he had constructed and the number of parish organizations he had founded. This was especially true after the collapse of the lay trustee system. The income of the new brick-and-mortar priest and his business responsibilities of administering ever larger and more complex parish structures, placed him, in his own and in his parishioner's eyes, quite above the rest."

Dolan notes that "with the demise of lay leadership in the parish, the focal point of the people's involvement shifted especially to the devotional arena, but also to the benevolent societies." Parish benevolent societies provided financial aid and other assistance for new immigrants. A variety of parished-based organizations emerged in the second half of the nineteenth century—the Holy Name Society; the Altar Society, through which women of the parish cared for the altar and its ornaments; the Knights of Columbus, formed to fight anti-Catholicism and to foster parish leadership; the Saint Vincent de Paul Society, a charitable organization.

The second half of the nineteenth century also saw the emergence of another major influence on parish life—the parochial school. Catholic schools served a twofold purpose. First, they were the primary means of education and religious education for Catholic children. Second, they were a refuge from the public schools, which were almost totally Protestant in orientation—

Catholic students were required to read Protestant versions of the Bible, recite Protestant prayers, and read textbooks containing passages ridiculing the Catholic faith.

The United States bishops, in the Council of Baltimore in 1884, required that every Catholic parish build a school within two years, a goal that spurred the expansion of schools even though it was never met. By 1900, about 40 percent of all Catholic parishes and about 50 percent in the Northeast had a parochial school. The parish schools were made possible by the availability of a large pool of people ready to work at less than subsistence wages—the nuns and a smaller number of religious brothers who did the teaching at the parish schools. The parish school also served another purpose—it increased the power of the pastor, who now had control of the school budget as well as the parish budget. In 1900 in the Northeast, as much as 50 percent of the parish budget was devoted to the school. Between 1880 and 1930, 1,945 new parochial schools were opened in the Northeast, with an enrollment jumping from 181,072 to 1,050,020. By 1910, more students were in parochial schools in Philadelphia than in the public schools of all but a dozen cities.

Methods of raising funds for parish operations also changed over the years. At first, parishes collected "pew rents" from families, fees for the use of a pew every Sunday. Later, subscription and pledge drives became more popular. A "revolution" occurred in the late 1910s and early 1920s with the introduction of the famous "envelope system" in which parish members were given envelopes for contributions for each Sunday and Holy Day. From the late nineteenth century on, parishes also raised money through social events like bingo and parish fairs. The annual parish fair became the social highlight of the year in many places.

REGIONAL DIFFERENCES

Because fewer than a third of American Catholics lived outside the Northeast and Midwest, there is a tendency to view the history of the other 30 percent of American Catholics as a smaller version of the church in New York or Chicago. But the church faced very different circumstances in different regions. Because of those different circumstances, parishes and their people had different experiences and different histories.

The history of the Catholic church in the South is particularly fascinating. Catholics made up a very small minority, and the Catholic church became a "peculiar institution" within an overwhelmingly Protestant culture. There were several reasons why so few Catholic immigrants moved to the South. First, most could not afford to get there because it was too far from their point of entry at New York City. Second, there was too much competition for cheap labor from blacks, first as slaves and then as freed people. Third, the Catholic church was such a small presence there that Catholic immigrants who wanted to be close to their church stayed away from the South. Finally, the Civil War brought such destruction to the South that it offered no hope for immigrants seeking work—and, in fact, the South made clear that it did not want the new immigrants.

The Civil War had a particularly strong impact on Catholic churches. The small number of priests, including those who had survived a yellow fever epidemic that took a large toll among the clergy, was reduced further when so many left parishes to serve as chaplains to the Confederate army. The Catholic church in the South launched an effort to serve newly freed slaves. Although largely unsuccessful, it did create a number of black parishes which served the same purpose as national parishes served for the immigrants.

Michael McNally notes that in the 1950s and 1960s "the drive for integration and equal rights for blacks had a curious effect on southern Catholicism and black Catholicism. It was an example of where the American dictum of the separation of church and state did not hold true. What was going on in the secular society was interpreted literally by Catholics southern bishops with a twofold effect. On the one hand, blacks were now on an equal footing in every Catholic church in the South. On the other hand, the drive to integrate all but destroyed an important black institution—the black parish and the black school. Although black Catholics supported the move to integrate in the public arena, they did not wish to abolish or 'consolidate' what they considered to be their parishes and schools. The move to close black parishes, influenced as it was from events in secular society, did not come from the grass roots, but from the hierarchy, who were concerned not only with cooperation with the political climate of civil rights of the times, but also with teaching the white Catholic community a lesson in social justice. The only problem was that nobody asked what the black Catholics might have preferred." In other words, the bishops' well-meaning support of civil rights served to deprive blacks of what were in effect their "national parishes" before these would have faded out on their own.

The south central region—Alabama, Arkansas, Kentucky, Louisiana, Mississippi, Oklahoma, Tennesse, and Texas—had a great deal in common with the south Atlantic region. The church in this region was primarily rural, and parishes stretched over vast areas, but it also had a rich ethnic diversity. Charles Nolan identified six major ethnic groups in this region: (1) the colonial French who settled the Mississippi Valley in the early 1700s, epitomized in the Catholic Creole life of New Orleans; (2) the early Spanish missions in Texas, augmented by Spanish colonials and their descendants from Mexico; (3) Africans and their descendants, mostly slaves—Louisiana's *code noir* legislation mandated that Catholic slave owners baptize their slaves, provide religious instruction, and keep their slaves' families intact; (4) American-born pioneers from the east coast who settled in Kentucky; (5) transplanted French settlers from Acadia and Santa Domingo who came into the region in the late eighteenth and early nineteenth century; and (6) the various Indian tribes living throughout the region. Like the Northeast and Midwest, the south central region had "ethnic" parishes, though many fewer of these after World War I. Some Irish, German, Italian, Czech, and Polish immigrants did settle in the region, but never in such numbers as in the North.

The West Coast was still very much a frontier area throughout the last half of the nineteenth century. There were only twelve parishes in Washington and Oregon in 1850. San Francisco was the only area with a regular parish life before 1880. Church development was hindered in part by a Wild West atmosphere—Los Angeles cancelled Christmas Eve Midnight Mass in 1856 because the Masses had become so disorderly. Jeffrey Burns reports that fire was a constant problem on the frontier: "Virtually every parish experienced the loss of one of its buildings due to fire during the frontier era."

Burns says the majority of churches in the frontier era were begun at the instigation of the laity. "Without the presence of a resident pastor," he says, "the laity took upon themselves the task of raising money for the building of a church. The general process was a subscription drive. Several laymen were given lists of various parishioners, whom they contacted and tried to induce to give donations for the future church. The subscription process was the most significant lay activity in the frontier parish. Once the church was built, the laity would then petition the bishop for a resident pastor."

Carol Jensen notes that the church's development was particularly slow in the intermountain region. "The late establishment of both civil and ecclesiastical boundaries and the continued shifting of ecclesiastical jurisdiction caused considerable confusion and delayed diocesan organization. Thus the first Catholic parishes in the Northwestern and Southwestern parts of this region were often the offspring of Indian missions established by Jesuits or Franciscans. The lack of early industrialization in the region, along with the boom and bust phenomena related to mining, delayed movement of the population from rural to urban settings. Thus despite the later development of several significant urban centers, Catholic parish life in this region has generally retained a rural missionary character."

Jay Dolan notes that in the West "the religious orders were used much like the Marines. They would come into places in Montana, Utah, Nevada, and they would establish the beachhead, planting the Catholic community in that particular area. Then, once the parish got established and there was a Catholic presence, the orders left town and the regular diocesan clergy came in and began to foster parish life."

The development of parishes in the South and West, as well as in Alaska, Hawaii, Puerto Rico, and the Philippines, was greatly helped during the first half of the twentieth century by the Catholic Extension Society, established in 1905 by Father Francis Clement Kelley. The society launched the home mission movement in the United States, raising funds to help the church in areas where it lacked personnel, organization, and financing. The society helped build more than seven thousand churches in addition to supporting the work of priests, seminarians, and missionaries. Carol Jensen concludes that "at a time in this nation's history when Protestant denominations were experiencing great evangelizing success on the American frontier (due in great measure to the support of their own home mission societies), Catholic parish life might not have been as firmly established in this region [the Inter-Mountain region] had it not been for the aid of this society." Jensen's conclusion about the region she studied holds up as well for the rest of the South and West.

TWO WORLD WARS

Remarkably little change took place in the internal life of Catholic parishes in the first half of the twentieth century, a time of remarkable growth for the institutional church. Two events in Rome were largely responsible for the quiescence of the laity in the early part of the century. In 1899, Pope Leo XIII issued a condemnation of "Americanism," or the "American heresy," charging that the church in the United States was discounting the importance of contemplative virtues, exalting the practical virtues, and watering down the purity of Catholic doctrine for the sake of conversions. Nine years later, Pope Pius X condemned "modernism," a series of heresies denying the existence of God, the inspiration of the Bible, and Christ's establishment of the church. The impact of both of these moves was to stifle dissent and intellectual creativity in American parishes.

Also in 1908, the Vatican declared that the United States was no longer mission territory. This cut off missionary funds from France, Bavaria, and Austria and slowed the development of the church in the South.

During the first half of the twentieth century, pastors continued to rule as monarchs; parishes continued to build Catholic schools; fund raising in the form of bingo, parish fairs, and other events became institutionalized; parish organziations continued to grow, with a new focus on young people as seen in the spread of the Catholic Youth Organization.

The First World War had a dramatic impact on American Catholics—it awakened a sense of their Americanism. Stephen Shaw points out that the impact was particularly felt by German Catholics who, feeling forced to choose between their German past and American present, suppressed their German ethnicity. While Italians, Poles, and others held onto their ethnicity until well into the second half of the century, German Catholic ethnicity effectively vanished with the war.

One practical result of the war was the establishment in 1917 of the National Catholic War Council to coordinate church activities. In 1919, the council was renamed the National Catholic Welfare Conference and continued to serve as a source of advice and coordination on religious, education, immigration, and social justice issues for the church. In 1966, it was renamed the United States Catholic Conference. (The old conference's initials—NCWC—were often said to stand for "Nothing Counts West of Chicago," reflecting the dominance of the Northeast and Midwest in the United States church.) The trend toward national consolidation continued during the Depression, when parish charitable organizations became linked.

The war also affected the ability of European countries to provide clergy to the United States. As late as 1914, eighty-nine percent of the diocesan clergy in New Orleans were foreign-born. The war hastened efforts to strengthen United States seminaries.

The major development affecting Catholic parish life in the first half of the century was congressional action in the 1920s to stop the flow of European immigration into the United States. This meant that, for the first time in more than a century, European immigration would no longer dominate the agenda of the American Catholic church. One practical result was the decreasing importance of national parishes; fewer were started, and many existing parishes were "denationalized." In 1930, 21 percent of the parishes in the Northeast were national; in 1960, this dropped to 17 percent.

By the 1940s, Catholic groups who had been in the United States for a long time, particularly the Irish and Germans, were moving solidly into the middle class. Four of five new churches built in the Northeast after 1940 were built in the suburbs.

World War II had a dramatic impact on Catholic parish life in several ways. First, the sacrifice of Catholic soldiers alongside other Americans went a long way toward dispelling anti-Catholic attitudes. Second, after the war, Catholics joined the move to the suburbs. Third, Catholics also took greater advantage than other Americans of the GI Bill and moved up in education and income levels. By the mid-1960s, the "immigrant" Catholics had the same levels of education and income as American Protestants. Finally, another result of the war and the postwar boom was that many Catholic soldiers from the Northeast and Midwest who had been stationed for a time in the South and West liked what they saw and began settling there after the war.

THE CONTEMPORARY PARISH

The postwar boom and suburbanization were accompanied by two other important movements. First, southern blacks poured into northern cities in search of jobs and often found themselves in "changing" neighborhoods inhabited by Catholic ethnics. Catholic suburbanization in the 1950s and 1960s contained an element of "white flight" from the inner cities. Second, large numbers of Hispanics began moving—both legally and illegally—up from Mexico, primarily to the Southwest, but also into large northern cities. The Mexican migration was accompanied by an influx of

Puerto Ricans into the northeast and—following Fidel Castro's takeover in Cuba in 1959—a flow of Cubans into Florida.

The year 1960 was a major turning point for American Catholics because it was the year the United States elected its first Catholic president, John F. Kennedy. Kennedy's election signaled a clear coming of age for the Catholic church and a substantial reduction in anti-Catholic bigotry—the Kennedy-Johnson ticket carried Alabama, Arkansas, Georgia, Louisiana, North Carolina, Texas, and West Virginia, a feat that only a decade before seemed impossible for a ticket headed by a Catholic.

The boost that Kennedy gave Catholics domestically was more than matched by the impact of the Second Vatican Council, which opened in 1962 and ended in 1965. While the Council said little about the parish as such, its decisions in a wide variety of areas made change in parish life inevitable. The Council also reflected a warm view of parish life—its byword was "pastoral," and the Council was suffused with an emphasis on the role of pastor serving his people.

Two Council actions were particularly liberating to American Catholics. The first was the redefinition of the church as the People of God. Once this was done, it opened up a new way of thinking about church life; it led to shared responsibility and shared decision making. The second important development was a shift of focus away from purely internal church life and out toward greater involvement with the world, from the local community to other faiths to world problems.

With the coming of the Council, Jay Dolan notes, "the longing for order, so central a feature of the Church in the immigrant era, has given way to a longing for pluralism."

The insular, conservative Catholic parish of the 1950s has been stereotyped, ridiculed, and recalled with fondness, but those same parishes were home to people becoming ripe for greater and more self-assured involvement in both their church and community. Dolan says that after the Council "the changes in parish life are obvious to any middle-aged Catholic—Mass in English; laypeople reading the Scriptures at Mass; women religious working in the parish not as parochial school teachers but as pastoral associates;

directors of religious education or social action programs; popular election of parish councils and laypeople distributing the Eucharist."

The parish council is a structure created after the Council and now mandated by canon law to collaborate with the pastor. While such councils are widespread, they are not uniformly effective. But the Council has, at least in theory and often in practice, clearly changed the nature of parish leadership: the pastor who tries to rule like a monarch will find himself at odds with a congregation expecting greater involvement in decision making.

Dolan notes, for example, that "many parishes have formed liturgical committees made up of priests, women religious and laypersons; rather than just one person—the priest—being responsible for the liturgy, a group of people now take an active role in planning parish liturgies. The same development has taken place in the areas of religious education, youth work and financial affairs; the ubiquitous committee form of decision-making has replaced the one-person rule of days past. In fact, parish consultation has become a cottage industry in the American Catholic community."

The post-Vatican II era was not without its pitfalls. Many pastors initiated changes in parish life suddenly, without proper preparation and education; others resisted any change. Parish "polarization" became a common story in the late 1960s and early 1970s, and many parishes suffered real trauma. But as Vatican II became institutionalized, there were fewer and less severe instances of the kind of parish disruptions common in the first decade or so after the Council.

Catholic parishes have gone through a number of changes since the Council, some flowing from it and some flowing from social change in America. One change, spurred largely by suburbanization, was that the Catholic school system stopped growing rapidly and began to shrink somewhat in the 1960s and 1970s. Catholics moving to the suburbs found better quality public schools than they had left behind in the cities, and they found that programs of religious education for children—the Confraternity of

Christian Doctrine (CCD), begun in the 1920s—were becoming more professionalized. Finally, public schools were much more pluralistic in nature and were no longer vehicles for transmitting an exclusively Protestant view of life and culture. The incentive to build new schools along with new parishes was simply not as great as it had been in earlier decades, and though new schools were built, there were proportionately fewer of them. Dolan points out that in many areas of the United States fewer Catholic schools existed in 1980 than in 1930. For example, Oregon had 54 Catholic schools in 1930 and 51 in 1980; Massachusetts had 275 Catholic schools in 1930 and 218 in 1980. In addition, with the exodus of many women from religious life after Vatican II, the responsibility for teaching in parochial schools fell more and more to the laity.

Immigration, while not returning to center stage in parish life, still made a major comeback as the church faced three new waves of immigrants—Mexicans and Latin Americans and Asians. Mexicans began crossing the border in increasing numbers; between 1970 and 1980, there were 1,868,000 new immigrants in California, more than 900,000 from Mexico. Large numbers of Vietnamese, Cambodians, and Thais also came to the United States after the end of the Vietnam War in 1975; many were Catholics, and Catholic agencies resettled about half of the Asian refugees. Finally, war and disruption in El Salvador, Nicaragua, Honduras, and Guatemala sent thousands of predominantly Catholic Central Americans north into the United States.

One of the most-heard words in the post-Vatican II parish is "renewal." Renewal takes many forms. Programs such as Renew, which emphasizes social action as well as spiritual development, are popular programs for whole parishes. Individuals seek renewal through prayer groups, Marriage Encounter, and Cursillo weekends. The Charismatic Renewal movement hit Catholic churches in the early 1970s and, after being met by initial suspicion, has become fairly institutionalized. Many of these movements are not parish based, but energize their members for more active parish life.

"In the 19th Century," Jay Dolan says, "the parish was the central gathering place for the people. This is where they manifested their beliefs and demonstrated their commitment to the Roman Catholic tradition. For many groups, such as the Polish in Chicago and the French Canadians in New Hampshire, even the neighborhood where they lived was named after the parish where they prayed. For these people and for many others, the parish was clearly a central neighborhood institution.

". . . . As the church developed in the 19th Century, other institutions such as hospitals, orphanages, schools and colleges were established. Nonetheless, the parish still remained the most important institution in the community. This was where the religion of the people was nurtured and strengthened; nineteenth century Catholic education is the story of the emergence of the parish school; through their parish organizations Catholics first learned the lessons of benevolence and social concern. It is no exaggeration to say that in the nineteenth century, the parish was the foundation of American Catholicism. Without it, everything else would have collapsed."

But what was true in the nineteenth century is not true today. In the 1980s, American Catholics are secure in both their Americanism and their Catholicism; they are part of the mainstream culture, and they carry their faith with them. The parish still serves as a source of community and faith, but it is no longer the foundation upon which all else depends. Today's Catholics turn to their parish as participants and leaders, using it as an outlet for their talents. The parish is no longer a haven from the outside community, it is a vehicle for relating to and transforming that community.

Dolan summarizes post-Vatican II parish life this way: "There have been changes in the deepest religious values. Once the Second Vatican Council sanctified the principle of participation of the people in the liturgy, the celebration of Mass and the sacraments were destined to change. The moment the Council defined the Church as the People of God, a change in thinking took place and eventually a change in acting as well; the concept of shared responsibility entered into Church life and with it came shared decision-making. These changes have been developing for close to 20 years and in ways most likely not envisioned by the bishops at the Council. History is like that. No one can predict the future, but release a powerful agent for change in a society undergoing rapid transformation and the future is unlikely to imitate the past."

The future for Catholic parishes in the United States offers the possibility for meeting an old problem with new solutions. One of the dominant realities of parish life today is the growing shortage of priests. The ratio of Catholics to priests, which decreased through the 1950s, has risen dramatically since then (see Table 1). In many dioceses, there were more Catholics per priest—often a great number more—in 1980 than in 1930. For purposes of comparison, we have added diocesan and religious order priests together in each diocese. This overstates the proportion of parish priests, because many order priests work in education or other areas removed from parish life. There are also a higher proportion of retired priests today than there were in 1930. Even with these caveats, however, the pattern is clear—the ratio of Catholics per priest decreased between 1930 and 1950 and then rose again through the 1950s, 1960s, and 1970s.

In the early days of Catholic parish life in America, there were few priests, many of whom were circuit riders, and lay people ran the parishes. As the church became more institutionalized and the number of priests increased, pastors took charge and ran a tight ship; the laity had to divert its leadership activities into parish organizations.

But two new forces are now at work. On one hand, the ratio of priests to lay people is decreasing, and in some rural and frontier parts of the country we are seeing a return of the circuit riding priest, this time traveling around in a battered Buick instead of a battered bronco. On the other hand, lay people are more educated than ever before and, under a new theology of church, commissioned to share responsibility in parish leadership.

The early days of the Catholic church in the United States saw lay people running parishes in the absence of priests. For a cen-

Table 1. **Catholics Per Priest**

DIOCESE	1930	1950	1960	1980
Boise, ID	322	355	459	697
Boston	892	721	702	809
Brooklyn, NY	1315	927	1194	1017
Chicago	987	799	737	943
Cleveland	946	774	881	1053
Denver	580	432	683	849
Fargo, ND	525	522	459	691
Great Falls, MT	477	555	636	665
Hartford, CT	1126	791	1088	1136
Indianapolis, IN	404	284	410	473
Los Angeles	616	1203	1187	1812
Newark, NJ	1418	1957	2067	2448
New York	852	584	649	705
Philadelphia	718	561	798	839
Portland, OR	280	281	349	762
Providence, RI	930	816	872	1019
St. Paul, MN	662	603	764	899
San Francisco	649	792	978	804
Santa Fe, NM	1374	1090	1122	1495
Seattle, WA	427	616	578	885

tury, priests took center stage and left the laity to "pay, pray, and obey." But, today, lay and clerical leadership are no longer predictably at odds with each other. Many are actively cooperating with each other in sharing ministry and leadership with the blessing of the pope and most bishops. A new era is just beginning.

NOTE

This chapter is based on the manuscript versions of regional histories of Catholic parishes written for the Notre Dame study and published as *The American Catholic Parish: A History From 1850 to the Present,* edited by Dr. Jay Dolan (Paulist Press, 1987). The authors and their respective regions were Dr. Jeffrey Burns (Pacific coast), Dr. Joseph Casino (northeast), Carol Jensen (intermountain), Rev. Michael McNally (south Atlantic), Dr. Charles Nolan (south central), and Dr. Stephen Shaw (the Midwest). Report 2 by Jay Dolan and David Leege was also used.

3. Core Catholics: The People in the Parishes

There are many ways to define a Catholic. Most public opinion polls define Catholics simply as those who identify themselves that way. Some studies have tried to differentiate among Catholics on the basis of Mass attendance, for example, by defining as "unchurched" Catholics those who attend church less than twice a year; about one person in four who identifies himself or herself as a Catholic falls into this category. The Notre Dame study worked with a different definition—what we called Core Catholics, or parish-connected Catholics. This was not by any means an attempt to say that these Core Catholics were better Catholics than those who were not active in parishes. It was simply an obvious way to define a group of Catholics in a study of parish life. If the goal is to study parish life, it is necessary to focus on Catholics known to parishes and served by them. (Just to make things interesting, two percent of Core Catholics were not canonical Catholics—that is, while they attended church, they had never been baptized. Many of these were blacks who attended black Catholic churches without officially joining.) For language and cultural reasons which will be explained in Chapter 5, we excluded Hispanic Catholics from our data. Many of them would certainly have been Core Catholics, but they were not included in this study. To sum up, then, for our purposes, Core Catholics were non-Hispanic Catholics who were registered members of parishes. More precisely, our sample of parishioners consisted of 2,667 Core Catholics from thirty-six representative parishes.*

---

*David Leege points out differences in sampling error between the survey of 1,099 parishes and the survey of 2,667 Core Catholics. He says the parish survey has a margin of error of three percentage points in either direction. It is not possible to

One additional point. Some people have suggested that we describe our parish-connected sample as "traditional" Catholics. It is true that Catholics who are registered in parishes and attend church regularly are somewhat more conservative than self-identified Catholics who attend church less regularly. But, as we shall soon see, our Core Catholics were by no means "traditional" in their attitude toward church teachings, policy, and priorities.

Since our sample of Core Catholics did not correspond to the United States Catholic population as a whole, we needed information about a national sample of Catholics for comparison. Unless otherwise specified, we used for comparison purposes data from national samples gathered by the National Opinion Research Center of the University of Chicago for its General Social Survey during the same year our study was done. We will first take a look at the demographic characteristics of Core Catholics and see how they differed from those of the general Catholic population.

DEMOGRAPHICS

Sex. Compared to Catholics at large, a higher percentage of Core Catholics are women. A full 63 percent of Core Catholics are women, about 6 percent higher than their representation in the national Catholic population. This reflects national patterns. Women are more likely to be churchgoers than men in all denominations, although among Protestants, women are even more

---

assert a similar margin of error for the Core Catholics sample, however. Leege says the Core Catholic sample does not sample Catholics randomly from "an enumerated Catholic universe." He notes that Gallup, National Opinion Research Center, and other national polls do not have this kind of sample, either. But, he says, because successive surveys by different research organizations show similar results, most social scientists are not concerned with the possibility of sample bias in Gallup, NORC, and similar surveys.

Leege used several other methods to verify the sample: "One is sample weighting. Through complex formulas, we have weighted our data by the reported size of each parish and proportion of the reported parish-connected Catholics in the United States. When we compared weighted findings with our unweighted findings, we found no principal variables with differences of greater than two percent between the weighted and unweighted findings. Therefore, we felt confident in the representativeness of our data."

likely than men to attend church—67 percent of regular Protestant attenders are women.

Age. Core Catholics are also considerably older than the general Catholic population. Nationally, the average age for adult Catholics in 42.6 years—younger than the Protestant average of 46 years. But Core Catholics averaged 49.3 years. This age difference reflects a "life cycle" effect: young people who are moving away from home, launching careers, and in many ways experimenting with their freedom, are much less likely to stay or become linked to a parish; as they grow older and begin to raise families, they gradually return to parish life. Certainly until a person reaches the declining years, church attendance increases with age.

Ethnicity. It is becoming increasingly difficult to identify Catholics by their ethnic background because each new generation adds to the number of marriages across ethnic groups. Even so, Core Catholics easily identify with their predominant ethnic backgrounds: Irish (23 percent), German (22 percent), French (13 percent), English (9 percent), Italian (7 percent), Polish (6 percent), other eastern European (5 percent), and Scandinavian (2 percent). Nine percent of the Core Catholics in our sample are black; this is much higher than the national representation of 3 percent, but it was done deliberately so we could generalize about black Catholics.

Denominational Background and Mixed Marriages. Ninety percent of current Catholics were raised as Catholics and 9 percent were raised as Protestants. 94 percent of current Protestants were raised as Protestants, 4 percent as Catholics. Catholics are more likely than Protestants to live in mixed marriages: 79 percent of married Catholics are married to other Catholics and 17 percent to Protestants, while 89 percent of married Protestants are married to other Protestants and 7 percent are married to Catholics. Mixed marriages within Protestant denominations—for example, Presbyterians to Episcopalians—are very common. There is little difference between the national sample and our sample of Core Catholics, of whom 80 percent are married to Catholics, 13 percent to Protestants, and 7 percent to those with no religious affiliation.

But there is a clear generational pattern to Catholic mixed marriages: the younger the Catholic, the more likely he or she will be married to a Protestant who remains Protestant. Among married Catholics over fifty, 14 percent are married to Protestants. Among those in their forties, the figure is 16 percent. Among those in their thirties, it is 21 percent. Among Catholics in their twenties, it is 28 percent. Not only are younger Catholics in a post-Vatican II atmosphere increasingly comfortable marrying Protestants, but also the Protestant spouses of young Catholics are less likely than in the past to convert to Catholicism.

Marital Patterns. Core Catholics are more likely to be married and, therefore, less likely to be single, divorced, or separated than the general population of Catholics. Nationally, 58 percent of Catholics are currently married, but 69 percent of Core Catholics are married. While 31 percent of Catholics nationally have never married, only 10 percent of Core Catholics never married. And while 13 percent of Catholics nationally are divorced or separated, only 6 percent of Core Catholics are now separated or divorced, with another 4 percent having remarried after divorce. In general, a disproportionate number of young singles in America are Catholic—41 percent of Protestants but 57 percent of Catholics under thirty—have never married.

Family Size. Not surprisingly, Core Catholics, who are older than the general Catholic population, have larger families. Core Catholics who have ever been married have an average of 2.82 children, while all Catholics who have ever been married have an average of 2.44 children.

Education and Income. Half of Core Catholics attended a Catholic grade school, 33 percent attended a Catholic junior high, 28 percent attended a Catholic high school, and 13 percent attended a Catholic college. American Catholics have had the same level of education as American Protestants for at least a generation. Catholics generally rank behind Presbyterians and Episcopalians in education and income and on a par with Methodists and Lutherans; non-Hispanic Catholics would rank closer to Presbyterians and Episcopalians. Core Catholics are particularly well educated. A full 60 percent have had some schooling beyong high school, including 7 percent who have done some graduate work and 9 percent who have advanced degrees; another 13 percent have completed college. The fact that Core Catholics have more education than Catholics at large is not surprising given that Core Catholics are older than the general Catholic population. But the magnitude of the difference—50 percent greater than the national average—suggests that those young Catholics who are not tied in to parish life are overwhelmingly working-class and minority youths. The same pattern holds up with income. Almost one Core Catholic in four—23 percent—had a family income above $40,000 a year, about one-third higher than the national figure.

Political Affiliation. In 1983, the year Core Catholics were sampled, Gallup surveys showed that 50 percent of Catholics were Democrats, 20 percent Republican, and 30 percent Independent. The Core Catholic sample found a virtually identical pattern, with 48 percent Democratic and 19 percent Republican. Since then, national surveys show that Republican affiliation peaked at about 32 percent in 1984 and has since edged downward. Since there seems to be no difference in political affiliation between Core Catholics and the national population of Catholics, we would expect the same pattern among parish-connected Catholics.

FOUNDATIONAL BELIEFS

Throughout our study of Core Catholics, we will be concerned with their beliefs—about the church and its teachings, its role in the world, and the role of the parish. But before we get to that level, we need to take a look at a different kind of belief—what social scientists call "foundational beliefs," our most deeply held values which shape all our other beliefs, including religious ones.

An important piece of work examining foundational beliefs can be found in *Religion on Capitol Hill* by Peter Benson and Dorothy Williams. Benson and Williams concluded that while legislators' religious affiliations did not predict the way they would vote on a particular issue, their basic worldviews—their foundational beliefs—would. Benson and Williams developed four basic pairs of foundational beliefs:

- For some people, religion is "agentic," focusing on their own needs and problems; for others, it is "communal," focusing on the needs of others and of the social community.
- For some people, religion is "vertical," directed at a relationship between a person and God; for others, it is "horizontal," directed outward toward other people.
- For some people, religion is "restricting," setting limits, boundaries, regulations; for others, it is "releasing," offering freedom to do new things.
- For some people, religion is a "comfort," a solace or assurance; for others, religion is a "challenge" to serve others and to transform individuals or society.

The Notre Dame study used the Benson-Williams themes to measure the way Core Catholics were represented on a scale with exclusively individualistic beliefs on one end and exclusively communal beliefs on the other. The parishioners' survey provided the basis for this measurement by asking people to answer three separate questions and to draw a line connecting those answers.

The first set of questions dealt with "The basic human problem" and asked parishioners to choose one of three responses or to reply in their own words. The choices were "Something lacking in my personal life"; "Separation of human beings from God"; and "Lack of human community or closeness between people."

The second set asked people to describe "The path to salvation" and to choose among these options: "Doing good works to earn God's favor"; "Trusting in God's free gift of forgiveness"; "Relying on the Church's sacraments to set things right"; and "Working hard to make our society better and more just."

The third set asked people to describe "The outcome of salvation" and to choose among "My life on Earth is changed; I feel fulfillment, meaning, joy"; "I will live forever with God in Heaven after I die"; and "The world will be changed so that people live together in peace and harmony."

An analysis of responses to these questions found that 39 percent of Catholics are exclusively individualistic in foundational belief; 18 percent are exclusively communal; 21 percent are integrated, defining their religious beliefs through both themes; and 22 percent either showed anomalous patterns or could not think in these terms about their religion.

The large proportion of Catholics with exclusively individualistic foundational beliefs is startling and sobering. It indicates that the church, which emphasizes communal symbols and values, faces constant tension with not only the individualistic impulses of American society, but with similar impulses among large numbers of its own members. To some extent, this impulse toward individualism is the product of four centuries of catechesis which emphasized growth in personal holiness and the individualistic nature of sin, confession, and absolution.

Whether a person's foundational beliefs are more individualistic or more communal do not affect his or her beliefs about the purpose of the parish itself; even those with individualistic worldviews described the parish's purpose in communal terms. But differences in foundational beliefs do affect participation in parish activities. Parishioners who scored higher on the communal dimension of faith are more likely to take part in social welfare and social justice parish activities and to say the parish should give a higher priority to helping the poor and changing unjust economic conditions. Parishioners who scored higher on the individualistic dimension are more likely to take part in public activities devoted to spiritual growth and renewal and to say the parish should be more active in reclaiming dropouts and converting the unchurched.

CHURCH POLICIES AND TEACHINGS

Earlier, we argued that it would be incorrect to describe our Core Catholic sample as "traditional" Catholics. Nowhere is that more clear than in their attitudes toward church policies and teachings on a number of important issues. Core Catholics are no less likely than unchurched or nonpracticing Catholics to make up their own minds. If they agree with the church on an issue, it is because the church position makes sense to them and they actively decide to agree. If a church teaching does not make sense to them, they will refuse to agree, no matter how often or how clearly or how authoritatively the church has spoken on it. The clearest example is the fact that Core Catholics are strong supporters of the church's teaching on abortion and almost equally strong opponents of its teaching on birth control.

Table 2 shows the opinions of Core Catholics on thirteen key church issues, of which seven are grouped as church policies and five are categorized as church teachings. The term *teachings* refers to ecclesiological and moral issues on which popes and councils have offered teachings, while *policies* signal variations in direction or emphasis that the church might take in implementing the objectives of Vatican II.

Table 2. **Core Catholic Opinion on Church Issues**

	STRONGLY DISAGREE (%)	DISAGREE (%)	AGREE (%)	STRONGLY AGREE (%)
Church Policy				
The church should become more people oriented; less concerned about its organizational structures and rules.	5*	19	50	26
The church should stress a personal, spiritual relationship to Christ.	1	3	54	46
The church should listen more to the voice of ordinary lay Catholics.	4	16	53	27

*Note: not all percentages total 100. Those that exceed 100 percent do so because of rounding; those that total less than 100 do not include "Don't know" or "No answer" responses.

	Strongly Disagree (%)	Disagree (%)	Agree (%)	Strongly Agree (%)
The church should put more emphasis on spreading the faith.	1	14	63	23
The church should make more effort to understand family life.		4	57	40
The church should put less emphasis on lay participation in the Mass or liturgy.	26	48	20	7
The church should follow through more on changes and guidelines that resulted from Vatican II.	4	22	64	10

Church Teaching

	Strongly Disagree (%)	Disagree (%)	Agree (%)	Strongly Agree (%)
The church should remain strong in its opposition to the use of contraceptives.	26	40	21	14
The church should remain strong in its opposition to abortion.	5	10	29	55
The church should liberalize its postion on divorce.	9	27	46	18
The church should allow women to become priests.	35	29	24	13
The church should allow married men to become priests.	17	24	36	23
The church should encourage Communion between Catholics and non-Catholic Christians.	10	29	49	22

Simply showing the percentage agreeing and disagreeing with these positions does not give us enough information about Core Catholics' beliefs about these issues. David Leege developed an "index of support" which offers greater precision in determining the degree of agreement with church positions. Leege used a scale of one to four points, with one point indicating strong disagreement and four indicating strong agreement. When the average score for Core Catholics is 2.5 or more, it means they agree with a position; the higher the average, the higher the level of agreement. We will now look more closely at attitudes on these thirteen issues in the order of greatest to least agreement. First, we will look at the church policy issues:

• The church should stress a personal, spiritual relationship to Christ (3.42).

It is not surprising that agreement with this statement was so high, because talk of a personal relationship with Christ and an emphasis on spreading the faith are socially desirable goals to which lip service is easily paid. There were very few differences in high levels of support for this goal, with women stressing it a bit more. Support among parish volunteers, staff, and pastors was just about the same as support among Core Catholics.

• The church should make more effort to understand family life (3.34).

The church has consistently emphasized family life, and Catholics look to the church for practical help with their families. Support is quite high among all groups; it is slightly higher among the divorced and remarried, indicating that this group feels it needs more help and recognition from the church than it is getting now. Volunteers, staff, and pastors expressed about the same degree of support as parishioners.

Core Catholics display a mixture of traditional and modern views on family life itself. They believe by 62 to 38 percent, that "strict, 'old-fashioned' upbringing is still the best way to raise children." But 73 percent do not agree that "the husband should have the 'final say' in the family's decision-making"; 53 percent do not agree that "it is best if the wife stays at home and the husband works to support the family"; and 98 percent agree that "both father and mother have the responsibility to care for small children."

• The church should put more emphasis on spreading the faith (3.07).

Groups scoring particularly high in this area are southern Catholics, those whose parishes are in small towns and cities, the elderly and widows, those who prefer a pre-Vatican II style of devotional life, and those who approach Sunday Mass as an obligation. Support for this direction was slightly higher among volunteers, staff, and pastors.

• The church should listen more to the voice of ordinary lay Catholics (3.03).

Women are more likely than men to support this view, and the more highly educated a parishioner is, the more likely he or she is to advocate more attention to the laity. In general, support for this position is high among educated suburbanites in their thirties through fifties who have had some Catholic education; among the divorced and remarried; those who are a little less likely to attend Mass every Sunday; and those who place a higher priority on social justice and helping the poor, ecumenism, improved liturgy, and adult education. The profile of Catholics who scored highest in this area is almost the opposite of those who say the church should put more emphasis on spreading the faith. The level of support for this position among volunteers and staff was the same as that among parishioners, although the level of support among pastors (2.94) was slightly smaller.

• The church should become more people oriented, less concerned about its organizational structure and rules (2.97).

The profile of Catholics scoring high in this area is almost identical to the profile of those saying the church should pay more attention to the voice of lay Catholics. The differences by gender and education are not quite as large in this group. Staff and pastors were even more likely than parishioners and volunteers to support a more people oriented church.

- The church should put less emphasis on lay participation in the Mass or liturgy.

Because this statement is phrased in the negative, we need to consider its reverse index, which is 2.92, indicating strong disagreement with the statement or strong agreement that the church should put more emphasis on lay participation. But of the Vatican II policy decisions, this issue seems to generate less consensus than the others. Those who value the participatory liturgy sparked by the Council differed sharply from those willing to retrench to more passive liturgies.

Those who favor participatory liturgies are educated suburbanites in their thirties through fifties who were currently in intact families; those who have attended Catholic schools; those who regularly attend Mass; those who like to share their faith with Catholics and non-Catholics alike; and those especially interested in social justice, ecumenism, and adult religious education. Participatory liturgy is particularly popular in areas like the mountain states where Catholics are few in numbers.

Those who favor a passive liturgy are those who live in ethnic concentrations in the northeast and Midwest; the elderly, widowed, and those who have never married; those who did not attend Catholic schools, do not attend Mass regularly, and much prefer the pre-Vatican II emphasis on Rosaries, Novenas, devotions to saints, and so on. Volunteers, staff, and pastors were considerably more likely than parishioners to support a participatory liturgy.

- The church should follow through more on changes and guidelines that resulted from Vatican II (2.81).

Support for this position is higher among women, the more highly educated, and those who attached importance to social justice, ecumenism, and improving liturgy. Volunteers, staff, and pastors were slightly more likely than parishioners to support greater follow-through on Vatican II.

It is somewhat surprising that support for further implementation of Vatican II reforms, although quite high, ranks last among policy options in our index. This reflects the fact that while three in four Core Catholics—74 percent—support further implementation, only 10 percent of those expressed strong agreement, while 64 percent simply expressed agreement. There are two possible explanations for this finding. One is a cooling of enthusiasm for Vatican II. But this is less likely in the context of our other findings, which indicate strong support for continued change in the church in the direction of the changes sparked by the Council.

The more likely explanation is that the Second Vatican Council, which ended more than twenty years ago, has become institutionalized. Catholics today are less likely to identify a more participatory style in liturgy and parish life specifically with the Council and more likely to simply accept it as the nature of the church itself. For Catholics in their twenties and thirties, identifying "the changes and guidelines that resulted from Vatican II" is an exercise in history because they have lived with those "changes" their whole lives.

Here is a more detailed look at responses concerning possible changes in church teachings.

• The church should remain strong in its opposition to abortion (3.35).

There is simply no recognizable group within our sample of Core Catholics who disagree with the church's opposition to abortion. Volunteers, staff, and pastors were even stronger in their support of the church's position. But this does not mean that Core Catholics will support public policy that outlaws all abortions. A separate question in our parishioners' survey asked, "Which of the following statements comes closest to your views about abortion?" Only 1 percent said abortion is always acceptable, and only 5 percent said it is acceptable under most circumstances. But only 26 percent said abortion is never acceptable. A full 69 percent— seven in ten Core Catholics—agreed with the statement that "abortion is acceptable under certain extreme circumstances, like a threat to the mother's life, rape, or incest." Core Catholics clearly reject abortion on demand or as a form of birth control. But they also reject an outright ban on abortion, viewing it as a medical option which should be available in extreme circumstances.

• The church should liberalize its position on divorce (2.72).

Usually, it is the younger, middle-class, educated Catholic who advocates change in church positions. But on this issue, the attitudes of young and old, educated and less educated are quite similar. Divorce, it seems, has touched every American family or circle of friends. The effort to find oneself again—with a new spouse, in the neighborhood, in the church—is a story widely known in the Catholic parishes of today's America. Support for change is strongest among the divorced and remarried and those who place a higher priority on social justice, ecumenism, and improving the parish's community life. Opposition is strongest among those who approach Mass as an obligation and felt the top parish priority should be evangelization.

There is considerable diversity of views on divorce among parishioners, volunteers, staff, and pastors. Parish staff (2.61 index) joined parishioners in supporting a liberalization of the church's position on divorce. But volunteers (2.42) and pastors (2.03) were strongly opposed.

• The church should encourage Communion between Catholics and non-Catholic Christians (2.82).

The ecumenical concern of Catholic parishioners is quite widespread. There are the usual differences with younger, suburban, educated Catholics more supportive and those with a pre-Vatican II devotional life and an emphasis on evangelization less supportive. On this issue, volunteers and staff were close to parishioners in attitude. But pastors—more likely to be influenced by existing church policies which place strict limits on intercommunion— were at odds with others in the parish and opposed intercommunion.

• The church should allow married men to become priests (2.65).

Core Catholics are quite comfortable with the idea of a married male clergy. The presence of married men as deacons is widespread in American parishes. Deacons administer the Eucharist with hosts previously consecrated by a priest; they perform home and hospital visits and lead many parish programs. To pragmatic American Catholics, it is a small leap from married deacons to married priests.

The more heavily involved Core Catholics were with parish responsibilities, the more likely they are to support a married clergy. The South is the only region where support falls short of a majority. Support is heaviest in the mountain, mid-Atlantic, and Pacific states where the Catholic population is more sparse, but is is also high in the ethnic enclaves of the Northeast and Midwest. Women are even more supportive of the idea than are men. Again, the age and education differences we have already seen many times are pronounced—the young and better educated are more likely to favor change, the older and less well educated are more likely to oppose it. Support for a married clergy was slightly higher among volunteers and staff, but pastors (2.36) were opposed.

• The church should remain strong in its opposition to contraceptives (2.23).

This response strengthens the argument that Core Catholics are anything but traditionalists—two out of three oppose the church's ban on artificial means of birth control. Support for the church's position is strongest in the South, Northeast, and Midwest. But only in the South does it (barely) reach majority proportions. Younger Catholics are strong opponents. Opponents of the church's teaching are not less faithful in Mass attendance and Communion practices. Supporters emphasize Mass attendance as an obligation, favor pre-Vatican II devotions, place a high priority on evangelization and the religious education of the young, and have little use for adult education, social justice, and ecumenism. Volunteers and staff joined parishioners in rejecting the church's teaching on contraception, but pastors (2.71) supported the church.

Andrew Greeley and others who have written about reactions to the 1968 encyclical *Humanae Vitae* are probably correct in describing it as a watershed issue in the American church. For a time, it contributed to the disillusion one generation felt with its church, although it was probably not the major reason for the decline in Mass attendance. Many middle-aged Catholics have come to identify with their church again despite its position on birth control. For younger parishioners today, the church's position on birth control is simply irrelevant. The long-term effect of *Humanae Vitae* was to help develop a loyal opposition in the American church—educated and active laypeople who feel it is appropriate for the church to offer moral teaching, but who will weigh it and consult their conscience and experience before deciding whether or not to accept it.

- The church should allow women to become priests (2.13).

While Core Catholics are comfortable with the idea of a married male clergy, they are decidedly uncomfortable with the idea of a female clergy. While opposition to this proposed changed is strongest in the South, it is weakest in the mid-Atlantic and mountain states. Generally, suburbanites are more accepting of women's ordination than those in rural areas or small towns. And, as usual, there is a very strong relationship with age and education: the young and educated are far more likely to favor this change than the older or less educated. While men and women are close to each other on this issue, educated women in their twenties to forties are considerably more likely to support women's ordination. Support is stronger among those with some Catholic education and those who give a high priority to social justice and ecumenism. Opposition is strongest among those who view Mass attendance as an obligation, favor pre-Vatican II devotions, and place a high priority on evangelization. Volunteers took the same position as parishioners on women's ordination. Parish staff were slightly more supportive, although a majority still opposed the change. Pastors (2.00) were strongest in opposition.

PARISH CONSENSUS

We now have a pretty good idea of what our national sample of Core Catholics looks like and believes. But it is not quite that simple. The national figures mask the degree of diversity which is found among parishes and within parishes. It is this mix of viewpoints which gives each parish its unique flavor. Social scientists have gotten so used to studying people in different groups—by race, age, sex, region, and so on—that they often lose sight of the fact that people live in communities and cooperate in various social institutions and that those institutions shape those views. Membership in a parish can have that kind of impact. It may be more important that I am a member of Saint Francis parish than that I am a sixty-four year old woman. And I may think more like a forty year old man from Saint Francis parish than a sixty-four year old woman from Sacred Heart. Put another way, a parishioner whose views are in a distinct minority at Sacred Heart parish might be in the mainstream at Saint Francis.

Social scientists gauge the degree of internal consensus within a group with a measure called the "standard deviation." Without going into technical detail, it is sufficient to say that the lower the standard deviation, the more people share a common viewpoint; the higher the standard deviation, the more they have different viewpoints. Parishioners' attitudes on church policies and positions differ considerably from parish to parish. For example, the parishioners in a small-town Texas parish barely favored a less rules-oriented church, while those at a suburban Colorado parish strongly favored a less rules-oriented church. Parishioners in an urban Mississippi parish opposed priestly ordination for married men, while the Colorado suburbanites strongly favored it. In the Texas parish, consensus was not high, while in the Mississippi and Colorado parishes, it was quite high.

Across the thirteen issues surveyed, average scores of parishioners in a parish ranged from a low of 1.63 to a high of 3.67 (with 2.5 being the point at which support for a position is indicated). The greatest gap came on the subject of ordaining married men. One parish had a 3.05, indicating strong support, and another had a 1.95, indicating strong opposition. The smallest gap came on the question of stressing a personal, spiritual relationship to Christ. The high was 3.74 and the low was 3.3, both indicating strong support. In general, there is more consensus among parishes on church policy issues than on specific church positions.

Parishes also differ from one another in their degree of internal consensus. The highest degree of consensus was found in a parish with a standard deviation of only .2; the lowest degree of consensus was found in a parish with a standard deviation of 1.16. The most consensus came on the question of the need for the church to understand family life; the least consensus came on the desirability of further implementing Vatican II changes. Consensus within parishes was higher on policy issues, lower on the more controversial position issues.

Do parishes that take a more extreme position than other parishes—whether they favor change or the status quo—suffer more dissension? Our data suggests no relationship between taking extreme positions and experiencing a lot of disagreement within a parish. And being consistent middle-of-the-roaders on church issues yields no higher than average consensus. Relative to the life of the rest of the church, parishes seem to have a life of their own. They pull together or tear apart on church issues about the same way they do on most of their internal life.

PARISHIONERS, PASTORS, AND MISPERCEPTIONS

How well do pastors understand their parishioners, and how well do parishioners understand their pastors? To answer this question, we asked parishioners for their estimates of how their pastors would feel about the issues on which they had just expressed their own opinions and asked pastors to estimate their parishioners' opinions. We used the average of parishioners' responses in each of thirty-five sample parishes to compare with the views of that parish's pastor.

Pastors and parishioners generally know each other's views, but some misperception exists. In 28 percent of the cases, pastors misperceived their parishioners' views; in 37 percent of the cases, parishioners misperceived their pastor's views. Pastors tended to overestimate their parishioners' commitment to implementing

Vatican II policies and to underestimate their commitment to further change in the church. Parishioners greatly underestimated their pastor's commitment to policy changes—such as greater commitment to spreading the faith, a more people-centered church, lay participation in the Mass, and understanding family life. They tend to overestimate their pastor's commitment to current church positions.

We found considerable diversity in misperceptions. Liberalization of divorce rules opens the widest gap between pastors and parishioners on church positions. In one-fourth of the parishes, the pastor and people occupy positions at different extremes. In thirty-two of thirty-six parishes, a majority of people wanted liberalized divorce rules, while only eleven of thirty-four pastors expressing an opinion favored liberalization. In general, pastors overestimated their parishioners' commitment to existing church teaching and parishioners underestimate their pastor's commitment to it.

On other issues we found the following:

- Parishioners are indeed very concerned about the church's lack of understanding of family life, but it is not their sole obsession, as many pastors seem to think. At the same time, parishioners' underestimated their pastor's commitment to meeting family needs.
- In almost half the parishes, parishioners fail to realize how deeply their pastor is committed to their participation in liturgies.
- Pastors tend to overestimate parishioners' commitment to a people-centered church, while parishioners tend to underestimate their pastor's commitment to such a church.
- In one parish in six, the pastor underestimates his parishioners' commitment to the church's opposition to abortion. But in another one parish in six, parishioners did not realize that their pastor believes that stance is too rigid.
- On contraception, thirteen pastors overestimated their parishioners commitment to the church's teaching. At the same time, fourteen pastors oppose the church's teaching, while parishio-

ners in thirteen of those parishes thought their pastor supported the church position. These figures suggest a quiet opposition within the clergy in these parishes on the contraception issue. Their people think the pastor supports the official teaching, but in reality, he does not. In a sense, higher church authority has bound the behavior of these pastors, but not their consciences. They are loyal to the church's hierarchy in that they do not voice their opposition; many seem also to hide their opposition from their flocks. Such pastors form another level of loyal opposition, side by side with their people.

- More pastors support a change in church bans on the ordination of women and married men than parishioners realize. While sixteen pastors supported ordaining married men and eleven supported ordaining women, parishioners in only two parishes knew their pastor supported ordaining married men, and in no parish did a majority of parishioners realize their pastor supported women's ordination. The same kind of quiet, loyal opposition exists on ordination issues as on the birth control issue.

- Pastors underestimated their parishioners' commitment to intercommunion with other Christians, while parishioners' overestimated their pastor's commitment.

- Pastors of black parishes are far more committed to change than are their people. On most church issues, black parishioners are oriented toward preservation of the status quo.

- Urban Catholics are not as liberal as their pastors believe them to be, while rural Catholics are not as conservative as their pastors perceived them to be.

- The length of time a pastor has served in a parish has very little influence on how accurately he will perceive the views of his people.

WHO IS A "TRUE" CATHOLIC?

As we noted earlier, our definition of Core Catholics is not an effort to define who is a "good" Catholic and who is not, or to define who is a "true" Catholic and who was not. But we did ask

Table 3. Core Catholic Opinion on "True" Catholics

IN YOUR JUDGMENT, SHOULD PERSONS BE CONSIDERED
"TRUE" CATHOLICS IF THEY

	Yes (%)	No (%)
Oppose nuclear disarmament	72	27
Commit "minor" crimes	56	42
Are married "outside" the church	55	44
Rarely go to mass	50	48
Live together outside marriage	37	61
Oppose racial integration	37	62
Practice homosexuality	32	67
Commit "major" crimes	31	67
Urge or undergo abortion	25	75

our parishioners to make that judgment based on a number of possible actions.

Some interesting findings emerged (Table 3). For example, 72 percent of Core Catholics believe it is possible to oppose nuclear disarmament and still be a "true" Catholic. But this does not mean that Core Catholics are unremittant hawks. To the contrary, some 90 percent support a bilateral nuclear freeze agreement between the United States and the Soviet Union. More likely, this response indicates that Core Catholics believe that one does not lose his or her status as a "true" Catholic by taking a political position.

The similar percentage holding that one can be a "true" Catholic after commiting minor crimes or marrying outside the church suggests that both are viewed as problematic, but not as matters which place one clearly outside the church. The virtual split on whether one can be a "true" Catholic while rarely attending Mass indicates that Core Catholics are divided on how serious a breach of church rules avoiding Mass constitutes.

The other five issues, where opinion is similar, are examples of behavior clearly considered sinful by the church and, not surprisingly, considered grounds for no longer being considered a "true" Catholic by our sample. But there are still some surprises here.

First, the strong support for racial integration is significant. It clearly shows that a combination of the church's emphasis on individual human dignity and the history of race relations in America have convinced Core Catholics that racial discrimination is a serious sin. Why the difference in attitude between those who "oppose racial integration" and "oppose nuclear disarmament"? The disarmament question is more clearly large-scale and political and is less personal. Opposing racial integration conjures up images of real people being the victims of face-to-face discrimination and is more easily identified as sinful behavior.

It is clear that to Core Catholics, urging or undergoing an abortion is the most serious basis for placing oneself outside the church. But the similarity in attitudes toward abortion, homosexuality, living together outside of marriage, racial discrimination, and committing a major crime is instructive. It suggests that even to Core Catholics, abortion is less a "life" issue than a "church teaching" issue and is not regarded as an issue which is a breed apart.

Core Catholics, then, seem to define their Catholicism on the basis of how well their behavior, as opposed to their beliefs, measure up to church teaching. But, at the same time, it is unclear just how seriously they view not being a "true" Catholic.

CONCLUSION

Though Core Catholics are older and more conservative than the Catholic population at large, they are clearly not a group in lockstep with their church leadership. About two-thirds of Core Catholics accept church positions on their own terms, often disagreeing with official church teachings. Core Catholics are increasingly affluent and educated. They have absorbed from American culture the values of independence, pluralism, and participatory democracy. They use these values in their work and social lives and see no reason to leave them behind in their religious lives. In short, the vast majority of Catholics active in parish life today have accepted and internalized the Second Vatican Council. They want even more changes in church and parish life, and they are ready to play a leadership role in bringing about those changes.

NOTE

This chapter is based on Report 2 by Jay Dolan and David Leege and Report 7 by David Leege and Joseph Gremillion. The authors of Report 7 acknowledge comments and criticisms from Sister Agnes Cunningham of Saint Mary of the Lake University, Mundelein Seminary; Father Timothy O'Connell of the Institute for Pastoral Studies, Loyola University of Chicago; and Professor Dean Hoge of the Department of Sociology, Catholic University of America.

The section on attitudes about who is a "true" Catholic is based on the parishioner survey responses.

4. Life and Community in the New Parish

One thing is certain about the post-Vatican II American parish: there is no such things as a "typical" parish. There is an almost dizzying variety of parish life, shaped by differences in geography, size, ethnicity, and leadership. The picture of Catholic parish life which emerges from the Notre Dame survey is at odds with many stereotypes of American parishes.

One stereotype, for example, is that all Catholic parishes are large. But the Notre Dame study found a vast difference in the size of Catholic parishes. The average parish had 2,300 parishioners, about 1,300 of whom attend Mass in a given week. (Nine percent of those at Mass come from outside the parish.) This is enormously different from Protestant denominations, where 50–75 percent of churches have fewer than 500 members. But, on one hand, 18 percent of American parishes have fewer than 500 Catholics living within their boundaries. On the other hand, 16 percent have more than 5,000 Catholics living within their boundaries, including 4 percent with more than 10,000. Another 22 percent have between 2,500 and 4,999 Catholics; 17 percent have between 1,500 and 2,499; 12 percent have between 1,000 and 1,499; and 16 percent have between 500 and 999.

The study also found a great variety from parish to parish in the density of Catholics in the general population. In a little more than one-third of United States parishes (36 percent), Catholics are estimated to make up less than 20 percent of the total population in the area—below their representation in the general population. In 20 percent, Catholics make up more than 60 percent of the population—well above their representation in the whole country. In 27 percent of parishes, Catholics make up 21–40 percent of the population; in 17 percent, between 41 and 60 percent.

Another stereotype is that Catholic parishes are found in the cities. They certainly are, and Catholics remain more urban than other denominations. But only thirty percent of the Catholic parishes are found in the cities themselves, twenty-four percent are found in the suburbs, and the rest in small towns and rural areas.

Based on General Social Survey data, David Leege estimates the number of Catholics outside cities and suburbs to be more than 14 million. This means that Catholics also make up the largest rural denomination in the country, with rural Catholicism being nearly as large as the entire membership of the largest traditionally rural Protestant denomination, the Southern Baptist Convention, and larger than another primarily rural denomination, the United Methodist Church.

The fact that contemporary Catholicism is both urban and rural is brought home by figures on how far Core Catholics have to travel to get to church. Twenty-two percent live less than a half mile from their church. Another 17 percent live less than a mile. But 28 percent live more than four miles from their church, including 6 percent who live more than 10 miles away.

Geographic distance has kept alive the parish mission. One parish in five still has a mission attached to it, and one in five of those have more than one mission.

The fading of ethnic identity is another stereotype of American Catholic life. While ethnic identity is clearly not as sharp as it was fifty years ago, Catholic parishes today retain an ethnic character. Pastors and parish administrators of the 1,099 parishes were able to name one dominant ethnic group: Irish—23 percent; German—21 percent; Italian—11 percent; Hispanic—8 percent; Polish—8 percent; French—5 percent; Black—3 percent; and Slovak—2 percent.

This ethnic heritage is responsible for the fact that 11 percent of United States parishes are still national parishes—a sharp decline from a few decades ago, but still a significant number. The vast majority of parishes—87 percent—are territorial, but a small

Table 4. **Core Catholic Attendance at a Particular Parish**

Reason	Respondents Mentioning This Reason (%)
Quality of pastoral care and concern provided by the parish priests	17
Qualities of friendliness and/or concern among members of our parish	14
The style of worship that is typical of the parish	7
The quality of the preaching at Mass	4
Many of my friends and/or relatives belong to this parish	3
The atmosphere of the church building itself	3
Opportunities for parishioners to participate in community service	2
The opportunity to get my children into the parish school	2
The "status" of the parish in the local community	1
Opportunities for becoming a lay leader in our congregation	1

number are described as "other." This group no doubt includes the nonterritorial "magnet" parishes established after Vatican II by some dioceses, including Chicago, to attract Catholics disaffected by the liturgy in their home parishes. Eighty-one percent of Core Catholics say they lived within the territorial boundaries of the parish they attend, 14 percent say they do not, and the rest are not sure. But while most Core Catholics attend Mass at their territorial parish church, only 56 percent give the fact that they live in a particular neighborhood as the reason for attending. They cite other reasons (Table 4) which indicated that they do not feel bound by the territorial limits of their parish.

When deciding which parish to attend, Core Catholics clearly take into consideration both the quality of priestly leadership and a welcoming atmosphere.

The stereotype of the Catholic parish usually includes a crusty

old pastor and a couple of eager young assistant pastors. Crusti-
ness and eagerness aside, that is not an accurate picture of contemporary parish life. Three percent of United States parishes have
no full-time priest and 52 percent have only one full-time priest.
Twenty-seven percent have two full-time priests, 14 percent have
three, and 4 percent have four or more. The average parish is
served by 1.7 full-time priests and .8 part-time priests, .3 permanent deacons, and .6 nuns. It employs 1.3 lay persons for pastoral ministry and has a parish council.

In the minority of parishes which have more than one full-time
priest, the age gap is not large. The survey found that the average
age of the oldest full-time priest is fifty-six, while the average age
of the youngest full-time priest is forty. Eighty-five percent of
parishes are staffed by diocesan clergy, fifteen percent by religious
order priests.

Only 36 percent of parishes have the services of a part-time
priest and 80 percent of those parishes have the service of only
one. Only one parish in four has a permanent deacon assigned,
but one-third have a religious sister hired explicitly for pastoral
services, including 12 percent with more than one nun performing
pastoral services. Only 5 percent of parishes have a brother em-
ployed in pastoral ministry.

A major change in Catholic parish life since Vatican II is the
appearance of the laity in parish ministry. Thirty percent of American parishes employ lay persons specifically for pastoral ministry—remarkably, about the same percentage hiring nuns for such
roles. One-third of the parishes with lay ministers have more than
one, including four percent who report having five or more.

EXPECTATIONS OF THE PARISH

What is a parish supposed to be? Catholics answer this question
in many different ways. One Catholic may see the parish as a
center for providing the sacraments; another may see it as a community of the People of God; another may see it as a vehicle for
the religious education of children. Most parishioners have a va-

Table 5. Core Catholic Opinion on the Purpose of a Parish

Theme	Respondents Mentioning This Theme (%)	Respondents Mentioning This Theme Exclusively (%)
1. Reference to parish as people of God, Body of Christ, family, community, fellowship of believers	42	9
2. Emphasis on charitable works; help for those in need	33	3
3. General reference to parish as a place for religious activity; spiritual enrichment	32	9
4. Reference to parish as a place offering worship and sacraments, liturgies	28	4
5. Emphasis on personal religious growth, faith, holiness, closeness to God, getting to heaven	26	4
6. Emphasis on religious formation, socializing children, evangelizing adults	25	3
7. Emphasis on preservation and propagation of the Roman Catholic faith	6	1

riety of expectations of the parish. Parishioners in the thirty-six parishes were asked, "In your own words, what do you think the purpose of a parish is supposed to be?" 13 percent gave no response; 33 percent gave one response; 34 percent gave two responses; 15 percent listed three; and 5 percent listed four or more.

The question produced more than sixty types of responses which were grouped into seven major themes. Table 5 lists the themes, the percentage mentioning those themes, and the percentage mentioning only a particular theme.

These findings clearly show that American Catholics are at home with thinking about the parish as the People of God and see the purpose of the parish as communitarian in nature—they expect the parish to build community, help the needy, and provide education. In particular, the percentage of Core Catholics viewing the parish in terms of the People of God is seven times the percentage viewing it as simply a means of preserving the institutional Catholic church.

PARISH SATISFACTION

Core Catholics are comfortable with the rhetoric of community and the People of God, and for many of them, that community is a reality. But for a disturbing number of others, it is not.

In general, Core Catholics are attached to and pleased with their parishes, giving them high marks for meeting their spiritual and social needs. Half—52 percent—say they are "very attached" to their parish, 41 percent say they are "somewhat attached," and only 7 percent say they are "not attached at all" to their parish.

These figures are tempered somewhat, however, by responses to another question which approaches the attachment question from a different angle. The question asked, "How upsetting would it be for you if you had to move and were forced to leave this parish?" 28 percent said it would be "very upsetting," 31 percent said it would be "mildly upsetting," 20 percent said it would be "not very upsetting," and 21 percent said it would be "not upsetting at all."

Responses to another question shed further light. This question asked, "How much of a feeling of community is there in your parish?" Fifty-seven percent said, "The parish shows a strong feeling of community"; 40 percent said, "The parish shows some feeling of community"; and only 4 percent said, "There is no feeling of community." (Totals add up to more than 100 percent because of rounding.) It is no coincidence that the percentage of those who say it would be at least mildly upsetting to leave their parish (59 percent) is virtually identical to the 57 percent who cite "a strong feeling of community" in their parish.

Core Catholics believe their parishes do a better job of meeting their spiritual needs than their social needs: 26 percent say their parish meets their spiritual needs "completely"; 59 percent "very well"; 14 percent say "not very well"; and only 2 percent say "not at all." These figures show a very high degree of satisfaction with the way today's parish meets the spiritual needs of parishioners, as should be expected of people who remain on the same parish roll.

But parishes are—not surprisingly—less successful in meeting their parishioners' social needs. Only 10 percent of Core Catholics say the parish meets their social needs "completely," although 46 percent say it meets them "very well"; 26 percent say the parish does not meet their social needs very well; and 18 percent say it does not meet them at all.

The lower level of satisfaction concerning social needs partially reflects the fact that most of the closest friends of Core Catholics do not reside within the parish. The survey asked parishioners to think of their five closest friends and then note how many live within their parish. Three in ten Core Catholics—29 percent— did not have a single one of their five closest friends living within the parish, 14 percent had one close friend, 17 percent had two, 13 percent had three, 9 percent had four, and 18 percent had five.

The survey did not determine how many close friends outside the parish were Catholics in other parishes and how many were non-Catholics. It is likely that the number of non-Catholic friends would have been fairly high. It would be safe to guess that a century ago, as Catholics turned to the parish as the center of their neighborhood and social life, most Catholics would have had almost all of their closest friends within the parish. That is not the case today as Catholics form part of the mainstream culture. One reason why the parish does a better job of meeting its con- gregation's spriritual needs than its social needs is that today's Core Catholics turn to the parish first for their spiritual needs. But when it comes to social needs, the parish offers just one option among many.

The fact that the parish is not the social center of its members' lives is reflected in the startling finding that three out of every eight Core Catholics say they never or seldom talk to other parish members in an "average" month. Only one in ten say they talk to other members of the parish daily, while more than half talk to other parishioners frequently.

Suburban Catholics are the least attached to their parishes. They had fewer "closest friends" from their own parishes and report fewer conversations with fellow parishioners. They are slightly less likely to say their parish meets their spiritual needs and substantially less likely to say it meets their social needs than Catholics in other types of parishes.

While the pastor is no doubt the key figure in the parish, only one Core Catholic in four report speaking with the pastor frequently. Forty-six percent say they seldom speak with him in an average month, and a full 29 percent say they never speak with him. Surprisingly, assistant pastors are even more remote—only 18 percent of those Core Catholics in parishes with an assistant pastor report speaking with him frequently during the course of a month.

These findings indicate a major gap between the rhetoric and reality of community for American Catholics. Taken together, they suggest that for about half of the Core Catholic sample, the parish provide a real sense of community. But for a large minority—possibly 40 percent—that community does not exist.

The Notre Dame study's on-site observers reflected this diversity in their comments. One said of a rural parish, "It's the most undynamic parish I've ever visited," and another described another rural parish as having "the most complete lack of community I've ever seen." But several noted particularly lively, close-knit congregations. One observer visited a low-income parish and marveled, "It's amazing what a poor community can accomplish."

PARISH PROGRAMS

Every Catholic parish offers Sunday Mass. But beyond Mass, parishes offer a wide array of other programs. The Notre Dame survey of 1,099 parishes asked for information about what "formally organized" programs they provided. This wording was intended to include information about programs run by lay volunteers as well as staff, but which are nevertheless a formal part of parish life.

Beyond Mass, the core of organized parish activity involves religious education, liturgical planning, parish governance, and specialized ministries to the sick, youth, and elderly. About half of the parishes have one or more of the following: social service programs, music and cultural activities, marriage and family programs, and/or a grade school.

About one-third of parishes provided programs to train parishioners for ministry and service, reach out to new members, and renew parish life. About one parish in five provided charismatic activity, social action programs, and ministry to the divorced. One in five has also used a parish consultant.

Table 6 lists the types of programs provided by parishes and the percentage of parishes providing them.

Table 6. **Parish Programs Surveyed**

PROGRAM	PARISHES PROVIDING THIS PROGRAM (%)
Religious education, grade school level	93
Religious education, high school level	84
Parish council	76
Liturgy planning group	72
Care of sick	71
Adult religious education	63
Youth ministry	62
Ministry to the aged	59
Social service (individual needs)	52
Music and culture	49
Marriage/family development	48
Prayer/reflection small groups	46
Parish grade school	45
Ministry training	37

Program	Parishes Providing This Program (%)
Parish planning process	34
Catechumenate (RCIA)	32
Evangelization	32
Parish renewal	29
Parish leadership training	27
Charismatic renewal	23
Ministry to divorced/separated	20
Social action (action for change)	20
Parish consultant	19

Obviously, not every parish provides every program. But did the programs provided form any discernable pattern? David Leege used techniques called "cluster analysis" and "discriminant function analysis" to divide the parishes surveyed into four basic types (see Table 7). Leege says that 83 percent of the parishes surveyed fit into these four types (some simply did not provide enough information) and that his models had better than a 90 percent rate in predicting where a parish would fit.

Table 7. **Parish Programs, by Parish Type**

Program	Type 1	Type 2	Type 3	Type 4
Mass	✓	✓	✓	✓
Religious education, grade school	✓	✓	✓	✓
Religious education, high school	✓	✓	✓	✓
Care of sick		✓	✓	✓
Youth ministry		✓	✓	✓
Liturgy planning group		✓	✓	✓
Adult religious education		✓	✓	✓
Ministry to the aged		✓	✓	✓
Music and culture		✓	✓	✓
Social service (individual needs)		✓	✓	✓

PROGRAM	TYPE 1	TYPE 2	TYPE 3	TYPE 4
Marriage/family development			√	√
Ministry training			√	√
Prayer/reflection small groups			√	√
Evangelization			√	√
Catechumenate (RCIA)				√
Parish renewal			√	
Ministry to divorced/separated				√
Charismatic renewal				√
Social action (action for change)				√
With parish school (%)	28	38	46	59

Type 1—The Simple Parish. Eighteen percent of the sample, 202 parishes, fall into this type, which provides little more than Mass and religious education for the young, what some have called a "sacramental service organization." 28 percent have a parish school.

Type 2—The Moderately Complex Parish. With 28 percent of the national sample (305 parishes), this is the most common type. In addition to sacramental service and religious education for the young, it is very likely to offer youth ministry, ministry to the sick, liturgical planning, music, adult education, ministry to the elderly, and social services to help the needy. It is more likely than the Simple Parish to have a school—38 percent have one.

Type 3—The Complex Parish. Nineteen percent of the parishes in the sample (205 parishes) fall into this type. In addition to the programs provided by the Type 2 parish, the Complex Parish is also very likely to provide prayer groups, evangelization, catechumenate, and ministry to the divorced and separted. Almost half—46 percent—have parish schools.

Type 4—The Very Complex Parish. Eighteen percent of the parishes in the sample (198 parishes) fall into this type. The Type 4 parish differs from Type 3 in three ways: (1) it is more likely to have a parish school (59 percent have one); (2) it is less likely to have programs dealing with marriage and family development, ministry to the separated and divorced, and ministry training; and (3) it is more likely to have prayer groups, programs for the elderly, parish renewal programs, charismatic renewal, and social action.

It is significant that almost four parishes in ten—37 percent—fall into the Complex and Very Complex categories. The variety of programs found in these parishes clearly reflected the influence of the Second Vatican Council.

What determines whether a parish will be Type 1, 2, 3, or 4? A parish's size and location and whether or not it has a school were important factors. Larger parishes offer a wider range of staff and programs; those programs tend to include a school. The larger parishes are located in cities and suburbs and are Type 3 and 4—complex—parishes. Type 1 and 2 parishes—less complex—are found in small towns and rural areas.

Leege found that certain social characteristics are related to the likelihood of a specific program being found in a parish. For example:

- Adult religious education is most likely to be found in black parishes (86 percent of parishes), the suburbs (75 percent), the middle and southern Atlantic states (75 percent), and the mountain states (70 percent); and less likely to be found in the Northeast (59 percent), the Midwest (62 percent), and rural parishes (45 percent).
- The suburbs are more likely to have marriage and family programs (60 percent) and ministry to the separated and divorced (33 percent); the cities are less likely (49 percent and 20 percent, respectively) and the rural areas least likely (36 percent and 11 percent, respectively).
- Parishes in which the largest ethnic group is Italian are more likely than other ethnic parishes to have programs for marriage and family development (59 percent) and ministry to the separated and divorced (33 percent).

But Leege says that these and other structures alone tell only a small part of a parish's story. "Environment counts," Leege says, "but the unique history of a people and its leaders count even more. Current parish patterns derive partly from the kinds of people served in a specific location, but they derive even more from the initiatives taken by leaders in the past. A pastor, a group of parishioners, a handful of sisters or brothers—any one may have contributed to a far different profile for a parish than its present social characteristics may dictate."

The study's close examination of thirty-six representative parishes bear this out. On several occasions, pairs of parishes operating within virtually identical demographic, economic, and social circumstances showed opposite signs of life. For example, one small, rural parish with a homogeneous community appeared barely functional, while another showed creativity, warmth, and vitality.

One irony which emerges from the Notre Dame study is that, while historians and sociologists point out the impact of personalities and conditions on differences between parishes, parishioners themselves are much less likely to see those differences. Only one in five Core Catholics who lives in a city with more than one Catholic church can cite "major differences" between these other Catholic churches and his or her own church. The others see minor differences (21 percent), no differences (10 percent), or say they are not aware of any differences.

PARISH PRIORITIES

The survey asked Core Catholics to rank ten items on a scale of 1 to 5, with 3 indicating the parish should give the item the same priority it is giving it now, 1 indicating the lowest priority, and 5 the highest (Table 8). Religious education and help for poor people within the parish rank at the top of priorities for Core Catholics. Help for the poor outside the parish and social change rank at the bottom.

Table 8. **Core Catholic Opinion on Parish Priorities**

ITEM	(LOWEST PRIORITY) 1	2	3	4	(HIGHEST PRIORITY) 5	AVERAGE (ON THE SCALE OF 1 TO 5)
Enhancing religious education of:						
Preteens	1*	1	44	17	37	3.88
Teenagers	1	1	36	19	43	4.04
Adults	2	3	51	18	27	3.64
Making converts and/or reclaiming church dropouts	5	6	36	19	34	3.70
Helping poor people within the parish	1	2	43	23	37	3.82
Helping poor people outside the parish	6	9	52	15	17	3.26
Improving the liturgy	4	6	54	19	17	3.40
Improving the social life of the parish	6	7	51	18	17	3.33
Improving contacts with non-Catholic churches within our neighborhood	7	8	48	19	19	3.33
Working to change unjust socioeconomic conditions	10	11	42	17	20	3.25

*Numbers are percentage of total response on that item.

While core Catholics ranked some items as higher priorities than others, it is also clear that they wanted their parishes to give higher priority to all the items surveyed. All items had average scores above 3, indicating sentiment in favor of more activity. Even on the lowest priority—working to change unjust socioeconomic conditions—more Core Catholics wanted their parish to give a higher priority (37 percent) than wanted a lower priority (21 percent).

PATTERNS OF PARTICIPATION

We have seen that Catholic parishes today provide a wide variety of programs. It is also true that Core Catholics are using those programs. Half—48 percent—took part in at least one activity beyond religious rites. Among parishioners, 21 percent took part in one activity, 15 percent in two, 8 percent in three, and 6 percent in four or more. Among the sample of parish leaders, 14 percent took part in one additional activity, 23 percent in two, 20 percent in three, 18 percent in four, and fully 25 percent in five or more.

Those Catholics who took part in parish activities showed a clear preference for activities of a social nature:

- 22 percent took part in social or recreational activities.
- 19 percent were involved in the liturgy, either on a planning committee or as a choir member, lector, or communion minister.
- 14 percent were involved in education.
- 12 percent were involved in some form of parish governance, such as finance, administration, bookkeeping, or committee work.
- 6 percent were involved in personal or devotional renewal.
- 4 percent were involved in social action, welfare, or justice issues.

One large gap between rhetoric and reality stands out in comparing expectations of parishes to actual parish life—the gap between those who cited charitable activity as a parish purpose (33 percent) and those who actually take part in charitable or social justice activity through their parish (4 percent). This, coupled with the fact that only 52 percent of parishes have social service programs and only 20 percent have social change programs indicates much needs to be done to bring rhetoric and reality together.

Core Catholics involved in parish activities spend a good amount of time at it: 30 percent spend an average of five hours per month on parish activities; 10 percent average fifteen hours; 3 percent average twenty-five hours; and 2 percent devote almost all of their discretionary time to parish work.

In nearly all categories of parish programs and ministries, married persons are more likely to be active than single persons. Those who devoted the most time to parish activities are the parents of children some of whom are under eighteen and some of whom are grown. Not surprisingly, these are the same people who feel their parish did the best job of meeting their own social needs. In a sense, participation is its own reward. But this pattern also reflects that parish life focuses on intact families to the detriment of singles.

There are also differences in participation levels among Core Catholics on the basis of their expectations of the parish. At one end of the spectrum are the postconciliar types, those who view the parish in terms of the Body of Christ or the People of God. Those in this group are most likely to be women and those age 18–49. At the other end of the spectrum are the preconciliar types who emphasize the church's hierarchy, institutions, and teachings. Those in this group are most likely to be men and over 50. The postconciliar types are most likely to participate in parish activities beyond Mass, including parish governance. The preconciliar types are the least likely to participate in activities beyond Mass. When the preconciliar types do participate disproportionately to their numbers, it is in parish governance and administration. The tendency for both groups to be active in parish governance suggests there is a potential for parish conflict based on different perspectives of what a parish is supposed to be, although this potential may be muted by the fact that so few parishioners are exclusively "institutional" in their definitions of parish.

One pattern of participation in parish activities stands out from all others—the intense involvement of women. The pastor remains the most influential figure in the parish, but beyond priests, Catholic parishes today are heavily dependent on the involvement of women. For example:

• More than 85 percent of those involved in ministry to the poor, sick, grieving, and handicapped are women, and social justice and peace efforts draw heavily on women.

- More than 80 percent of CCD teachers and sponsors of the catechumenate are women.
- More than 80 percent of members of prayer groups are women.
- More than 75 percent of those who lead or take part in adult Bible study or religious discussions are women.
- Almost 60 percent of those involved in youth and recreational ministries are women.
- 52 percent of parish council members are female.
- 58 percent of those identified as the most influential leaders in the parish in our 36-parish survey were women.
- Half of the lectors and at least half of the eucharistic ministers in our survey were women.

It is no exaggeration to say that women form the backbone of Catholic parish life in the United States today.

PARISH VITALITY—AND THE STAYING POWER OF BINGO

In addition to examining the extent of parish programs and participation, the Notre Dame study examined the vitality of those programs. One finding that emerged is a bit of a surprise at first glance, but not upon further reflection. The plain fact is that after the Sunday Mass, the most popular, well attended, and vital parish activity is—bingo.

Many church leaders have long been embarrassed by the prominent role which bingo plays in parish fund raising. In an age of "passion for excellence" management even in parishes, it seems a bit awkward to have a significant part of the parish budget come from a game of chance. Recently, Cardinal Joseph Bernardin of Chicago urged parishes to replace bingo with a system of tithing. Bishop Warren Boudreaux of Houma-Thibodeaux, Louisiana, has taken a more urgent approach, demanding that parishes phase in a total ban on the use of bingo, gambling, and parish fairs and festivals as fund raisers over a ten-year period.

Bingo ranked behind only Sunday Mass in attendance; 60 percent of those in the parish survey listed bingo as the second-most attended activity. When parishioners were asked what activities best exemplified their parish's vitality, 29 percent picked bingo, again ranking it behind only Sunday Mass. Bingo was disproportionately mentioned as a source of vitality in Type 2 and type 3 parishes. One percent of parishioners are involved in running bingo.

What accounts for the staying power of bingo? It combines raising money for the parish with socializing. Anyone in the family can go; people can go with friends. It provides an evening's entertainment at less than the cost of a movie. A small-stakes game of chance is offered among friends in a safe atmosphere.

But bingo also has deep roots in the history of the American Catholic parish. Bingo is a weekly version of the annual parish fair that has provided both a major social event and a major fundraising event for the past century. In one northwestern parish in the Notre Dame study, bingo was held twice a week from five thirty to midnight, with a lay coordinator and eighteen volunteers. People came from outside the parish to play. In 1982, bingo raised $138,000 for the parish, and, along with $25,000 in concessions and food sales, paid the operating expenses of the parish school.

Finally, bingo performs another useful service. As parishes offer more programs, parish life tends to become more fragmented. Married couples with children don't meet single members of the parish. Parishioners active on social action don't come into contact with members of the liturgy committee. The old and the young often have nothing in common. The parish is one institution which brings people from a variety of backgrounds together. Apart from the Mass itself, no other parish institution does it better than bingo.

Bingo might seem out of place in the post-Vatican II church, but it has shown remarkable staying power because of its deep-rooted tradition in the United States church.

The importance of social activities can be seen in findings about involvement in other parish activities. After bingo, the best-attended activities were adult religious education (mentioned in 21 percent of parishes); religious education for children (20 percent); parish school activities and sports (17 percent); Lenten services and devotions to the Blessed Virgin Mary (12 percent); and parish social and fraternal organizations, such as the Knights of Columbus (10 percent).

Activities listed as a source of parish vitality were children's religious education (25 percent), parish school activities and sports (24 percent), adult religious education (20 percent), social and fraternal organizations (18 percent), the parish council and other forms of parish governance (11 percent), parish social services (10 percent), social justice programs (8 percent), liturgical preparations (7 percent), and youth ministry (7 percent).

The survey of 1,099 parishes asked respondents, "What factors have contributed to the development of these vital elements of your parish?" The major reasons offered were good leadership and participation by the people: 20 percent cited high involvement by the laity; 19 percent each picked the quality of staff and the unique feeling of community in their particular parish; 18 percent cited an appropriate response to people's needs; 15 percent cited the parish council and lay involvement; 14 percent cited the support of the people; and 13 percent cited the vision of parish leadership.

When asked to name the kinds of things their parishes do best, parishioners offer a different perspective than their pastors: 28 pecent of pastors cited worship and prayer as things their parish does best, while 11 percent cited social functions. But parishioners are about equally divided between citing education and community. One-fourth cite religious education, CCD, and the parish school. Another one-fourth cite social functions, building community, and a friendly atmosphere, including a friendly pastor. Only 5 percent cite Mass as one of the things the parish does best; 3 percent cite "everything." These figures suggest that while pastors are more likely to think of the parish as a center of worship, their parishioners are more likely to think of it in terms of communal life and education.

PARISHIONER NEEDS, PARISH OPPORTUNITIES

As we have seen, parishes already provide a great variety of programs. But if Core Catholics had their way, they would provide some more.

The survey asked Core Catholics to tell where they would go for help if they had a particular problem—their pastor or parish staff, friends, or professionals outside the parish. The survey also asked them if they would turn to the pastor or parish staff for help on the same problems if help were available. What emerged was an "opportunity gap" revealing areas in which large numbers

Table 9. **Where Core Catholics Turn for Help**

NEED/PROBLEM	TURN TO PARISH (%)	TURN TO FRIEND (%)	TURN TO PROFESSIONAL (%)	WOULD TURN TO PARISH IF POSSIBLE (%)	OPPORTUNITY GAP
Religious education for children	84	1	2	86	2★
Religious education for myself	83	2	3	85	2
Support for faith	78	9	1	79	1
Premarital counseling or marital renewal	74	3	9	78	4
Counseling at time of sickness	53	18	19	64	11
Opportunities to serve others	48	21	18	60	12
Death of a family member	46	44	4	49	3
A place to express doubts and fears without judgment	44	34	11	49	5

*Numbers indicate increase in percentage points of Core Catholics who would turn to the parish for help if such help was available.

Need/Problem	Turn to Parish (%)	Turn to Friend (%)	Turn to Professional (%)	Would Turn to Parish if Possible (%)	Opportunity Gap
Severe marital problems	39	11	37	60	21
Family problems	37	24	26	51	14
Unwanted pregnancy	32	15	35	47	15
Handling of painful memories	30	43	16	39	9
Alcohol/drug abuse	13	7	67	50	37
Severe money problems	7	28	53	26	19
Unemployment	5	25	56	30	25

of Core Catholics would turn to their parish for help if it were available (Table 9).

American parishioners appear willing to place heavy demands on their pastors and parish leaders—and, ultimately, on themselves, given the nature and composition of contemporary parish leadership.

The first four problems listed in the table are either "religious" in nature or are traditional family concerns in a Catholic setting. All are central to what people expect of parishes and what virtually all parishes do. The next group of problems—from counseling at time of sickness to handling painful memories—represent a kind of middle ground. They are not strictly "religious," but they deal with emotional and spiritual traumas. The parish is likely to be a source of help, but, in some cases, help is just as likely to come from friends or professionals. The third set of problems—psychological and financial—are seldom seen as problems the parish can handle.

The opportunity gap shows little ground for improvement on issues such as religious education, but there is an opportunity for greater parish service on family matters, financial matters, and alcohol and drug abuse.

The high proportion of parishioners who would turn to the parish for premarital counseling and marriage renewal (74 percent) plummets when it comes to severe marital problems, family problems, and unwanted pregnancy. David Leege says, "It almost seems as though parishioners are saying, 'The parish is the right place to set our marriage on course and to make modest adjustments in marital communication, but it has little to offer when we face truly difficult situations in our marriages.' And, given the Opportunity Gap measure for the latter, they are saying, 'We wish the parishes offered more to ride out the tough situations.' "

There are some differences in attitudes toward approaching the parish for a variety of needs:

• Younger Catholics of higher educational and income attainments who are currently raising families are less likely today than were their immigrant grandparents to seek orientation from the church for many of life's problems. They would turn to friends and professionals, rather than to the parish staff. Today's middle-class Catholics are deeply involved in a world of civic and religious institutions outside the parish—colleges, hospitals, agencies, retreat centers, business associations, professional groups. These offer professional services better than those a home parish could provide. Still, the parish remains a source of individual help—by referral to a good professional by pastor or staff member, by good counsel from fellow parishioners, by mutual support in crisis.

• Blacks are far more likely than whites to turn to the parish for help with socioeconomic problems. This is true even for middle-class blacks, who are more likely than whites of similar education and income levels to turn to the parish for help in this area. One explanation may be that many black Catholics are converts from churches with a strong tradition of ministering to the needs of the whole person. Another possible explanation is that black Catholics are more likely to live in neighborhoods where poverty and unemployment are more visible problems than in white suburbs, towns, or rural areas.

- Parishioners in the suburbs place heavy demands on their parishes for spiritual services, but are far less likely to turn to the parish for socioeconomic services; urban parishioners are just the opposite.

CONCLUSIONS

Despite the immense variety in Catholic parish life in the United States today, several themes do emerge which reflect the state of the contemporary parish. First, Core Catholics treat the territorial parish the same way they treat church teaching. They follow church teaching when they agree with it. Similarly, only a bare majority of Core Catholics attend their local parish simply because it is their local parish. Almost half of those surveyed cite other reasons, indicating that they want to attend a parish that meets their individual needs. The fact that only a relative handful of Core Catholics, aside from those attending national parishes, regularly attend Mass outside their local parish reflects both habit and a sign of satisfaction with the local parish.

This desire for a parish that meets individual needs reflects another theme. For today's Catholics, the parish is not a service station for the sacraments. They turn to the parish for community, services, and opportunities to serve—and, to a remarkable degree, they are finding them. This sense of community, expanded parish programs and services, and increased opportunity for participation are responsible for and fed by an explosion of lay participation in parish life.

The promise of Vatican II and the reality of the post-Vatican II parish have fueled expectations among Core Catholics of even more opportunities for participation and service. Core Catholics want more from their parishes—they want more in terms of help with personal problems, such as dealing with family and chemical dependency problems, and they want more opportunities for ecumenical and social service activity. On a practical level, with no end to the clergy shortage in sight, expanded lay ministry is the only way to meet these expectations.

Parish vitality is related to a sense of community, and that community is fed by opportunities for social contacts among parishioners. Parishes will never be as successful in meeting their parishioners' social needs as they are in meeting spiritual needs, and, frankly, there is no reason why they should be. But a major fact of life in the post-Vatican II parish is that a good social life improves a congregation's spiritual life.

Finally, one clear sign of the commitment to Vatican II goals is the emphasis in American congregations on parish renewal. Of the 1,099 parishes surveyed, 29 percent had made use of some "packaged" parish renewal program like Renew. One in six of the thirty-six parishes studied in depth were using such a program at the time of the study.

NOTE

This chapter is based on Reports 3 and 4 by David Leege and Thomas Trozzolo and Report 8 by David Leege. The authors of Report 4 acknowledge comments and criticisms on drafts from Professor Dean Hoge of the Department of Sociology, Catholic University of America and Father Philip Murnion of the National Pastoral Life Center in New York. Leege acknowledges comments and criticisms on Report 8 from Hoge, Murnion, and Professor Richard Schoenherr of the Department of Sociology, University of Wisconsin-Madison.

Some material in this chapter is drawn from the on-site, ethnographic reports on thirty-six sample parishes.

5. The Hispanic Community and the Parish

The United States Bureau of the Census estimates that there will be 20 million Hispanics in the country legally by 1990. The Hispanic population reached 17 million in early 1986, having grown by 16 percent during the period 1980–85. By comparison the United States population overall grew by only 3.3 percent during the same five years. The census bureau explains this exceptional increase in Hispanic population as the result of high fertility and "substantial immigration to the United States from Mexico, Cuba, and other Spanish-speaking countries." By some estimates, an additional 2 million Hispanics are in the country illegally. Historic new immigration legislation enacted by Congress in late 1986 should regularize the status of numerous undocumented Hispanics and provide for hiring aliens under "resident permits" which could lead to citizenship. The Hispanic population is likely to increase even further due also to fresh waves of refugees from war-torn Central America.

The vast majority of Hispanics in our country have had some relationship with Catholicism, as family tradition, religio–culture, or institution. Most direct contact with the church occurs at the neighborhood level, through parish and school. The Catholic nature of Hispanics and the importance of the parish are reflected in the fact that the United States bishops, who have long supported immigration reform, have committed their parishes to set up offices to help regularize the status of those granted amnesty under the immigration bill.

Given the distinctive character of Hispanics as a religio–cultural community, their history, and continuing influx from Latin America, the Notre Dame study chose to exclude Spanish-speaking congregations in its in-depth analysis of thirty-six parishes. The need of Spanish language questionnaires and on-site visitors, plus research scholars familiar with Hispanic culture and religiosity, figured heavily in this decision.

But the survey of 1,099 parishes produced some valuable information about Hispanic parishes, and we have supplemented that information with material from other sources. Fifteen percent of the pastors and administrators surveyed listed Hispanic as the first or the second largest ethnic grouping within the parish. Projecting this percentage to all United States parishes—19,300 in 1986—it appears that more than 2,800 Catholic congregations have significant numbers of Hispanics. These large-scale figures do not show, however, the percentage of Hispanics in each parish, whether this be 10 or 20 percent, or 40 percent and more.

The use of Spanish in weekend liturgies is a clear indication that Hispanics do constitute a significant proportion among parish members. Thirteen percent of the parishes surveyed in the Notre Dame study reported that Spanish was regularly used in parish services. When this 13 percent is extrapolated to our 19,300 parishes nationwide today, this indicates that in about 2,500 United States Catholic churches a Sunday or Saturday evening liturgy is conducted in Spanish each weekend.

THE LOCAL HISPANIC COMMUNITY

Mexican-Americans account for 60 percent of the Hispanics in the United States—about 10.3 million people, compared to 2.7 million Puerto Ricans and 1 million Cubans. The remaining Hispanics come from a variety of backgrounds. Most of the United States parishes with significant Hispanic presence are located in six states, in which over 75 percent of all United States Hispanics reside. These are California and Texas with about 5 million and 3.3 million respectively; New York and New Jersey with 2.3 million taken together; and Florida and Illinois with about 1 million Hispanics in each. That is a six state total of around 13 million

Hispanics. (These figures are rounded extrapolations updated from the 1980 census.)

Dioceses of these states have established offices to provide their parishes with a wide variety of services adapted to Hispanic presence and culture. These offices also make sociological studies and surveys for deepening their understanding of Hispanic religiosity, demographics, and societal settings, for developing a more effective ministry. Such studies were pioneered by Father Joseph Fitzpatrick, S.J., in New York during the 1950s, and by the Mexican-American Cultural Center in San Antonio, directed by Father Virgil Elizondo of that archdiocese. Since Vatican Council II, more regional centers for Hispanic pastoral research have been established, each covering several states and providing survey data and scholarly insight to the Hispanic apostolate.

This chapter will take a quick glimpse at five areas with large Hispanic concentrations, to introduce the pastoral concerns, approaches, and problems of their local churches: New York City, Chicago, Miami, California, and Texas.

New York City and its environs have more than 1.5 million Hispanics, of whom more than half reside in Manhattan and the Bronx, territory of the New York Archdiocese. In 1982 the Archdioceson Office of Pastoral Research published a weighty report, *Hispanics in New York: Religious, Cultural and Social Experiences,* which presents findings from twelve-hundred interviews and numerous case studies, plus scholarly analysis of popular religiosity, cultural change, and familial, social, and economic situations. This study found that one of every three Catholics in Manhattan and the Bronx is Hispanic and that only 10 percent were born in the United States, while half were born in Puerto Rico and a fourth in the Dominican Republic. About 83 percent are Catholic and 9.3 percent are Protestant, mostly pentecostal or evangelical, while the rest are unaffiliated. Most changes to Protestant affiliation occurred in the States.

A reflection question in *Hispanics in New York: Who Are We?* the guidebook put out by the archdiocese for follow-up discussion, asks, "How do we relate to our parish?" In summary, New

York Hispanics responded: "When we were asked to describe the good experiences that we have had with the Church in New York, half of us said we felt welcome there . . . one out of every six of us, however, did say that some priests are cold and unconcerned. About one in ten mentioned that the church provides very little help with social problems. . . .

"One-third of us talk to the priests in our parish, and nine out of ten feel that the parish priest is important to our family. Eight out of every ten of us feel it our duty to contribute to the church. In spite of good experiences and attitudes, only one out of every fifteen of us belong to a church society or organization. We just aren't very involved in this way. Most of us are satisfied with the Sunday Mass. . . . One quarter did say that we dislike or just put up with Mass in English. Hardly anyone said this about Mass in Spanish."

In Chicago, a *Parish-Based Report on Pastoral Ministry to the Hispanics* published in 1983 said, "The 1970s will be remembered as an era of Hispanic population explosion . . . even more alarming is . . . [the fact] that census figures can be viewed as a 'guesstimate.' It is widely known that for various reasons the Hispanics in all of America tend to be undercounted."

Countries of origin for Hispanics in the city of Chicago were Mexico for 60 percent, Puerto Rico for 27 percent, Cuba only 3 percent, and 10 percent from other countries, according to the 1980 census. While this census counted only 499,000 Hispanics in Cook and Lake counties, which composed archdiocesan territory, Chicago's Office of Hispanic Apostolate puts the 1986 number at 800,000 Hispanics. This means that more than 30 percent of Chicago's Catholics today are Hispanic. By the year 2000 that proportion will probably approach one-half, due to new arrivals and because in 1985 more than a third of the city's Hispanics were fourteen years old or younger—with their child-bearing years ahead—compared with less than one-sixth of whites being that young.

The archdiocese provides the names of 89 Chicago parishes in which "Spanish Masses" are celebrated on weekends and the time of each; 20 parishes have two, three, or more such liturgies. There are 116 Catholic schools in Chicago with 5 percent or more Hispanic students enrolled. Of these, 80 schools have a Hispanic student body exceeding 20 percent; 43 exceed 50 percent, and 24 schools reach 80 percent Hispanic, with 11 ranging above 90 percent.

The Hispanic population of the Miami area is about two-thirds million, of which 70 percent are Cuban. Almost all have arrived since the revolution under Fidel Castro in 1959. Another one-third million Hispanics are scattered around south Florida, with about 100,000 in the Tampa area. The influx of the Cuban-born into Florida was massive and sudden. In a few months the first wave raised pre-Castro numbers more than 300 percent to about 125,000 Cubans by 1960, on up to half a million by 1970, and more than 800,000 in the 1980 census. Many were wealthy and middle class; the exceptional "Mariel boatlift" of May 1980, however, brought 125,000 Cubans of lower socioeconomic status.

The Catholic diocese of Miami was created only in 1958, the area having remained till then under the pastoral care of sleepy St. Augustine, 300 miles to the north. Miami is now a thriving archdiocese, after what seems in hindsight serious organizational procrastination by the Vatican. The hustle and heart with which the Miami diocese improvised as a one year old, with the pell-mell arrival of empty-handed refugees in repeated waves, brought quick ecclesial maturity. Scores of new parishes were created; priests quickly learned Spanish; social services of exceptional scope were organized to meet massive emergencies; lay leaders came forward—for church and society.

In a "Pastoral Letter to the Spanish-speaking of Our Community," Archbishop Edward McCarthy in 1983 acclaimed the enrichment brought to Miami by the refugees "who emigrate to our beaches, moved by political and economic crises of their own nations. . . . I admire the capacity for work of the Hispanics of South Florida. I admire their initiative, their commercial and industrial success." While citing the danger of overassimilation as a people, the archbishop also warned against isolation. He urged,

"Integrate yourself in the life of our civil and religious community. Take part in public life. Support capable and upright candidates. Prepare yourselves to serve in public office, sacrificing perhaps more lucrative personal interests."

On the down side, McCarthy lamented that only 10 percent of Miami Hispanics practice their faith, due especially to "shortage of priests in their countries of origin." He therefore challenged "practicing Hispanic Catholics to share their Faith with all their brethren . . . who live on the fringe of the Church." This, he said, must become the pressing concern of "leaders of our Catholic movements and organizations and Lay Ministers who work in this portion of the Church."

California counts about five million Hispanics, more than 20 percent of its population. While a few descend from the original settlers, most by far are of Mexican forebears via migration northward which began in the early 1900s, increased steadily with the spread of irrigated agriculture in the 1920s and 1930s, then surged upward during labor shortages of World War II, and presses on today. While 3.5 million are concentrated in southern California, in and around Los Angeles and San Diego, about 800,000 Hispanics live in the Bay Area. The dioceses of San Francisco, Oakland, and San Jose have therefore well-developed ministries among them, as have those of Sacramento, Fresno, Stockton, Monterey, and elsewhere.

During the 1960s and 1970s, the best known Catholic of California was a Mexican-American farm worker, Cesar Chavez. Indeed, he must be nationally ranked among the top lay leaders of his generation, alongside the Kennedy brothers and Dorothy Day. However great his contribution to the status of *los braceros* nationwide, his more significant contribution might well be support for the poor and voiceless which he aroused among the bishops of California, and in turn from the National Conference of Catholic Bishops.

In 1986, the Los Angeles archdiocese, with more than 2.5 million Hispanic Catholics, launched a five-year pastoral program for Hispanics under its new archbishop, Roger Mahony. It began with "a one-to-one visitation contact" with every Spanish-speaking person "to communicate a personal message of welcome from their local Catholic community." Mahony has called on every Catholic organization and renewal movement to make home visits a priority. Family life, youth, and the "close link between faith and Hispanic culture" provide pastoral focuses.

Social ministry has been central to the Los Angeles program. Mahony has formed a task force to oppose eviction of illegal aliens from federal housing, declaring, "There are no illegal aliens in the Catholic Church." Centers for immigrants are being set up to provide temporary housing, food banks, job and medical referrals, and immigration counseling (needed to implement the new immigration law with its complex process and documentation requirements).

Mahony has urged parishes to add paid Hispanics youth ministers to their staffs and has encouraged Catholic schools to provide night classes in literacy, citizenship, and English. These have become more needed in the wake of strong California voter approval in November 1986 of state Proposition 63, which instructs the legislature to "take all steps necessary to insure that the role of English as the common language of the State of California is preserved and enhanced." A national poll taken through 1,618 telephone interviews in June 1986 by *New York Times*/CBS News asked this question: "In parts of this country where many people speak a language other than English, should state and local governments conduct business in that language as well as in English, or should they only use English?" Of total responses, 60 percent said English only, 36 percent wanted other languages as well. The breakdown by race gave these percentages: whites were 64 percent for English only, with 32 percent permitting other languages, and blacks favored English alone by the close ratio of 50 to 44 percent. Reversing the white ratio, however, only 34 percent of Hispanics chose English alone, while 63 percent wanted other languages as well.

Bilingualism will continue for some decades in church and society where Hispanics predominate or have significant concentrations, such as Miami, Texas, southern California, New York, and inner-city Chicago. Very likely American Catholicism as a whole will be influenced for generations to come by Hispanic culture and its faith expressions. Even if second and third generations acquire English as their first language, the steady entry of Latin Americans will probably replenish and increase Hispanic presence into the middle of the twenty-first century—due simply to population growth in the south, especially in Mexico, and near-stable demographic levels in the United States. Only when Mexican birth rates drop significantly will the flow northward wane.

Some contend, in fact, that along the Rio Grande an irreversible Mexican-American matrix has already developed, with roots which are economic as well as cultural, and should be given political expression by both countries. Along its 800-mile course between El Paso and the Gulf, the river banks are alive with a million and a half residents who pass repeatedly, even daily, from one side to the other. More millions make their way from the deep interior of Mexico seeking work in the north. In the fiscal year 1985–86 more than one and a half million crossed the border, were caught by the United States patrols, and sent back. Meanwhile, from Brownsville west to Tijuana, businesses move capital from the United States and Japan into Mexico, construct factories along its upper rim, pay pittance wages, then move their products across the frontier for sale in the States or transshipment worldwide.

Church leaders along this permeable border are generally sympathetic to this stream of people. Some Christians offer them shelter and "sanctuary" in churches and hiding places, providing a modern version of the Underground Railway which abolitionists operated for American slaves before the Civil War. The million refugees from war-torn Central America, over half from El Salvador, are a special concern for the Sanctuary movement.

It wasn't until the 1970s that the church began naming Hispanics as bishops of key dioceses, such as Santa Fe and San Antonio. The latter is of special importance because Archbishop Patricio Flores is identifiably Mexican-American, born in his own archdiocese of Mexican migrants. About half of San Antonio's million inhabitants are Hispanic, and around three million reside in the dozen other dioceses of Texas. For example, Mexicans number about one-third million in El Paso; more than a half million in the down river cities of McAllen, Laredo and Brownsville; about two-thirds million in the environs of Houston; and one-third million each in the Corpus Christi and Dallas–Fort Worth areas. Besides these urban concentrations, almost another million of Mexican descent are scattered from Austin to Victoria and Waco and over a hundred other counties of Texas.

Since Vatican II, San Antonio in particular and Texas dioceses in general have shown aroused pastoral creativity adapted to the Mexican culture. Above all the whole liturgy can be celebrated at last in Spanish, with vigorous congregational participation. And lay leaders have joined clergy and religious in developing impressive movements of renewal, such as *Cursillos de Cristiandad,* which have influenced in turn many "Anglo" parishes and lay groups nationwide.

THE PARISH AND HISPANIC POLITICAL LEADERSHIP

The church has long been a source of political leadership for American blacks. Congregations have provided a training ground for leaders and a vehicle for mobilizing voters. The most important black leader of the twentieth century was a minister—the Reverend Martin Luther King, Jr. Many black ministers have gone into politics, and no one running for mayor of a major American city can hope for success without making an appearance at a black church.

It is not likely that the parish can play an identical role for Hispanic Catholics. The church's hierarchical structure, in dramatic contrast to the looser structure of, for example, black Baptist churches, places some limits on political involvement. Similarly, the new Code of Canon Law's ban on partisan political involvement by priests prevents Hispanic priests from going into politics.

But even though Hispanic parishes cannot play the same role as black parishes in training political leaders and influencing political decisions, they do play some role. The strong support for Cesar Chavez's leadership of farm workers in the 1970s came from Mexican-American Catholics based in parishes. Since then, community organizations with parish support have been major vehicles for Hispanic political influence. For example, in San Antonio, COPS (Community Organizations for Public Service) has tapped into parish leadership to form a network of Hispanic organizations which has become a major force in Texas politics, holding politicians accountable for the impact of their decisions on the poor and successfully lobbying the state legislature for increases in funding for education and health programs.

Hispanic parishes will not duplicate the performance of black churches in the political arena. But they are already following the model set by ethnic and geographic parishes in the political assimilation of earlier waves of Catholic immigrants.

NATIONAL SURVEY OF HISPANIC CATHOLICS

By far the most thorough survey of "the Hispanic Catholic in the United States" is reported in the book of that title, published in 1985, by the Northeast Catholic Pastoral Center for Hispanics, New York, which conducted the study. In 230 pages with 270 tables, authors Roberto Gonzalez and Michael LaVelle present with clarity, currency, and conciseness the "Socio-Cultural and Religious Profile" of Catholic Hispanics nationwide, which the subtitle promises. Bilingual interviewers conducted telephone interviews with 1,010 persons who indentified themselves as Hispanic Catholics. Fifty-five percent preferred using English while 45 percent chose Spanish. They were randomly selected from within the country's forty metropolitan areas, each of which contains more than 50,000 Hispanics.

Places of birth of the 1,010 respondents were 42 percent in the United States, 30 percent in Mexico, 9 percent in Cuba, 5 percent in Puerto Rico, and the rest in a score of other countries. By age, 31 percent were under thirty years, 45 percent are between thirty and fifty years, and 24 percent older. Twenty-eight percent have six grades or less of schooling, while 24 percent are high school graduates, and 28 percent range from "some college" to graduate school. Asked about annual household incomes, 24 percent refused to answer. Of the 766 who did respond, 23 percent reported household incomes below $7,000 a year, with 42 percent between $7,000 and $20,000, and 35 percent above $20,000—of whom 7 percent reported $40,000 or more.

The vast majority of Hispanic Catholics, 83 percent, state religion to be a "very important part of their lives," and only 3 percent say it is "not important." Notably, 91 percent of those answering in Spanish call religion "very important," while only 76 percent of English respondents did so; however, 18 percent more of the latter answered "somewhat" important. By education, about 90 percent of grade school level respondents said religion was "very important" compared to 83 percent of high school and 79 percent of college graduates. Both of the last named, however, added "somewhat important" answers to bring their "important" totals to 94 percent. This leaves less than 6 percent of high school and college graduate Hispanics who class religion as "not important."

Concerning specific Christian beliefs, 88 percent responded positively that "I believe in God who cares, loves and forgives me, and I have no doubts about it." Another 9 percent affirmed that same belief "sometimes," with some doubts. Responses to these two statements were by age, 84 and 13 percent for those under thirty years; and by education, 87 and 9 percent for college graduates. Ninety-four percent of the whole sample affirmed their belief that "Jesus is the Son of God made man, i.e., truly God and truly man," with 93 percent concurrence by both high school and college graduates.

Four areas of sexual morality were probed: abortion, artificial contraception, premartial sex, and marital infidelity. Table 10 gives in percentages the degree of acceptance of Catholic moral teaching, by the total sample, by age, and by education level.

Table 10. **Hispanic Catholic Opinion on Sexual Morality Issues, by Age and Education**

	ALWAYS WRONG (%)	SOME DOUBTS (%)	NOT WRONG (%)
Abortion, total	68	16	13
Under thirty years of age	59	21	16
Thirty to fifty years of age	67	16	14
High school graduates	69	15	12
College graduates	48	27	30
Contraceptives, total	40	19	37
Under thirty years of age	31	18	48
Thirty to fifty years of age	37	22	37
High school graduates	40	19	39
College graduates	27	27	45
Premarital sex, total	63	—	—
Under thrity years of age	51	19	26
Thrity to fifty years of age	64	14	17
High school graduates	62	13	18
College graduates	45	21	33
Marital infidelity, total	94	—	—
Under thrity years of age	92	4	3
Thirty to fifty years of age	93	5	2
High school graduates	93	4	3
College graduates	97	2	1

The respondents were also asked, "In your opinion, what are the two most serious sins?" Murder with 49 percent, adultery with 19 percent, and stealing with 11 percent were the top three responses. Missing Mass was listed by only .9 percent, and changing religion by .2 percent. Concerning religious practices, 48 percent said they attend Mass regularly on Sundays and Holy Days, 22 percent once or twice a month, and ten percent only once a year or never. Reception of Communion monthly or more often was reported by 41 percent, several times a year by 20 percent, and never or almost never by 25 percent. Motivations given for attending Mass were to worship and praise God, 50 percent; to fulfill an obligation, 14 percent; to ask favors and blessings, 5 percent; and by habit and custom, 5 percent.

Many questions were asked about "religious folk practices," not institutionally required by the church, but having a religio-cultural tradition among Hispanics. Notably, 28 percent have a "home altar," 45 percent keep "candles in the house under a religious image," 62 percent "sprinkle holy water," and 25 percent "burn incense." All these, we should stress, are external acts and situations occurring within the home, and involving the family as a whole. Strong observance of individual practices are also reported: "wearing medals, crucifixes, scapulars," 73 percent; saying the Rosary, 62 percent; giving thanks before meals, 58 percent; prayer "upon waking or before going to sleep," 82 percent; and 61 percent report that they read the Bible.

The place of Mary among Hispanic faithful is legendary. It is no suprise that 78 percent of all respondents said that she is "very important" in their lives (nine out of ten Spanish-speaking and seven out of ten English language respondents.) Given the prevalence of Mexicans among United States ethnic groups, an expected high of 35 percent gave La Guadalupe as the "preferred title" of Mary; however, the generic "Virgin Maria" is used most often by another 41 percent.

Of the seven Catholic sacraments, respondents were asked, "which *three* are most important to you?" Answers were Baptism, 88 percent; Matrimony, 56 percent; Eucharist, 54 percent; Confirmation, 39 percent; anointing the sick, 18 percent; penance, 17 percent; and holy orders, 4 percent. Among the welter of data about sacraments, two elements must be highlighted: even those married civilly or in a non-Catholic church ceremony rated Matrimony as second only to Baptism in importance, and 52 percent of all respondents stated they had been to confession during the past year.

What about the relation of Hispanics to the local church, at the level of the parish, its priests, staff, and people? Respondents were asked to identify the *two* best "positive experiences of the church in your area," among a list of eight possibilities. The four top answers were "felt welcome," 31 percent; "priests friendly," 25 percent; "sensitive to culture," 11 percent; and "feeling of community," 10 percent. Another 5 percent reported "helpful with social problems," while only 3 percent cited help with spiritual problems.

The mirror question about negative experiences in the local parish was also asked. Strikingly, 70 percent stated that none of the eight complaints listed applied. Only 3.3 percent "felt rejected," while 4 percent reported both insensitivity to culture and unconcerned priests. The top criticism was lack of help with social problems, by 5 percent. Another 3 percent complained that the Mass was not in Spanish.

And to what extent is the Mass available in Spanish? That pastoral situation is positive to an astonishing degree. Of the 1,010 persons questioned, 55 refused to answer or "didn't know." Of the 995 who did respond, 88 percent reported that a "service in Spanish is available where they attend Mass." Further, 94 percent of Spanish-speaking respondents said a service in their language is available. This availability varies by region: 26 percent in the Midwest and 15 percent in the northeast report lack of Spanish services, compared with 10 percent in the Far West, 9 percent in the Southwest, and only 3 percent in the southeast. This spread may show an expected relationship to the degree of concentration of Hispanics in each region; they are more scattered over the Midwest and densely gathered in Miami and south Florida.

Hispanics are not very familiar with church developments since Vatican II. Fifty-five percent said they had "never heard of" the Council, while 65 to 78 percent know nothing of the lay apostolate or parish councils, liberation theology or base communities, Medellin or Puebla. Only 50 percent, however, had not heard of the peace pastoral of the United States bishops, while 53 percent knew nothing about *Cursillos de Cristiandad* or Charismatic Renewal. In classifying "modern church developments" by degree of importance, the United States peace pastoral received the highest rating across the board; perhaps the media coverage it has gotten figures in this ranking. Media attention could also account for the "three religious leaders of today" identified most often by the respondents. After Pope John Paul, named by a whopping 65 percent, the next three are Billy Graham with 7 percent, Jesse Jackson and Mother Theresa with 5 percent each. Local bishops were named by 20 percent, but no one had more than 3 percent of the mentions.

FUNDAMENTALIST CHURCHES AND PROSELYTISM

The nationwide study by the Northeast Pastoral Center clearly documents that "proselytism" among Hispanic Catholics "by alternative religious groups" is spread through all regions of the United States. Gonzalez and LaVelle found 79 percent responded affirmatively to the interviewer's question: "Have you ever been approached here in the United States by such groups as Evangelicals, Pentecostals or Jehovah's Witnesses to convert to their religion?" This high percentage of approaches was found, the report continues, "in almost every single category examined: among the younger and older respondents; among those in all of the income and education brackets; among all of Hispanic ethnic and generational groups."

Asked whether "you have ever considered yourself a member of one of these types of religious groups?" 96 percent answered never, while 4 percent said they "had at one time been involved in a religious group like the Evangelicals, Pentecostals or Jehovah's Witnesses."

Several hundred tiny pentecostal and evangelical congregations in New York slums reportedly provide for some 200,000 members a base-community experience comparable to that which animates South American *barrios* and *favelas*. Angelo Falcon, director of the Puerto Rican Institute, New York, believes that fundamentalist churches, including store fronts, are beginning to mobilize Hispanics in a way analogous to the black Baptist experience. He explains, "People feel they are playing a bigger role in the community, that they are becoming islands of stability and refuge for folks trying to survive economic dislocations and political difficulties."

A rosy future for fundamentalism among northeast Hispanics is foreseen from the rapid increase of ministers. Thousands are now being trained. The Mizpa Bible Institute, for example, opened in the Bronx in 1980 with fifty students. Five years later the seminary had four hundred enrolled, mostly Puerto Ricans preparing to become full-time pastors or lay ministers who promote social engagement. Most fundamentalist zeal is first expressed through street preaching and door-to-door witnessing, which calls together a fresh little flock.

Some experts believe that the appeal of fundamentalism is as much sociopsychological as theological. "More important than belief is belonging," says the Episcopalian director of Hispanic ministry in Jersey City, Dr. Jaime Vidal, who has a doctoral degree in theology from Fordham University. "Newly arrived Hispanics feel uprooted and abandoned, that the rules and mores of their old world do not apply here. Someone with a strong emotional charge appears and offers love, community support and an alternative to a world that no longer exists, and they move quite easily into that new matrix." The Fordham Jesuit who pioneered Catholic concern for and research of New York Hispanics in the 1950s, Joseph Fitzpatrick, concurs that fundamentalists have sought "to play a community service and advocacy role," which makes them known to the new immigrants, "who then begin to come to church." Some fundamentalists groups regularly welcome new arrivals from Puerto Rico and the Dominican Republic at airports.

It must be recalled that in this survey, only Catholics were interviewed. Each respondent to the telephone call was first asked whether he or she identified himself or herself as Catholic. If the answer was negative, the conversation ceased. This being the case, the survey does not provide an estimate of the true extent to which Hispanic Catholics have defected from the Church and joined other religious groups. However, in their effort to reach at least one thousand Hispanic Catholics, the interviewers spoke with Hispanics who stated they were not Catholics. These totaled "approximately 15 percent of all Hispanics who were reached. This datum suggest that, perhaps, approximately 15 percent of the total Hispanic population in the nation is non-Catholic."

Some significant percentages of Hispanics are, of course, not affiliated with any church. The survey of Hispanics in the New York archdiocese, cited earlier, indicated a ratio of 83 percent Catholic and 17 percent non-Catholic, of whom about 9 percent were Protestant and around 8 percent unaffiliated. The nationwide ratio of 85 percent Catholic and 15 percent not, offered from the Gonzalez-LaVelle report, corresponds closely with the New York finding. Based on the expected number of at least 20 million legal Hispanics in the United States by 1990, we could project the ratio to about 17 million Catholics and 3 million non-Catholics, about half Protestant and half unaffiliated.

Gonzalez and LaVelle believe that, despite "sectarian challenges" to their Catholicity, "the vast majority of Hispanic Catholics in the nation would have to be regarded as solid, socio-cultural, and institutional Catholics from the perspective of the traditional style of Latin American Catholicism. In the long run, the greater challenge to the Hispanic American Catholic identity may come from individualism, materialism, and secularism, rather than from the sectarian challenges examined in this study."

BISHOPS PASTORAL ON HISPANIC PRESENCE

In 1983, the National Conference of Catholic Bishops issued a pastoral letter entitled *The Hispanic Presence: Challenge and Commitment*. It opened by stressing the church's "vast body of teaching on culture and its intimate link with faith. . . . Hispanic Catholicism is an outstanding example of how the Gospel can permeate a culture to its very roots. But it also reminds us that no culture is without defects and sins. Hispanic culture, like any other, must be challenged by the Gospel."

Among cultural and religious values which Hispanics especially cherish and exemplify, the bishop cited respect for the dignity of each person regardless of social status; reverential love of family life which embraces its roots and identity in "the entire extended family"; a marvelous "sense of community that celebrates life though 'fiesta' "; deep appreciation for "God's gift of life, and an understanding of time which allows one to savor that gift"; and "authentic and consistent devotion to Mary, the Mother of God."

After brief historic and demographic facts, the bishops came directly to the harsh socioeconomic reality: "In general, most Hispanics in our country live near or below the poverty level . . . the Hispanic community as a whole has yet to share equitably in this country's wealth—wealth they have helped produce . . . Hispanics participation in the political process is limited by ecomonic and social underdevelopment. Thus Hispanics are severely under-represented at decision-making levels in Church and society."

Leaving major socioeconomic concerns to their 1986 pastoral on the American economy, the bishops in this letter focused on Hispanic ministry. They recognized that "the survival of faith among Hispanics seems little less than a miracle," because so often "the institutional Church could not be present" through ordained clergy, vowed religious, organized parishes, schools, and services. It was for most Hispanics "their family-oriented tradition of faith" which provided the dynamism and channel for preserving and handing on the faith, generation to generation. However, the United States bishops warned, "Let us not depend only on that tradition today; every generation of every culture stands in need of being evangelized."

The bishops urged for today's ministry in our country "the *pastoral de conjunto,* a pastoral focus and approach to action arising from shared reflection among the agents of evangelization." Adapted from the 1979 Conference of Latin American Bishops, held in Puebla, Mexico, this conjoined pastoral ministry recognizes both "the sense of the faithful and hierarchical teaching as essential elements" for expressing the faith. It also favors "group apostolate." Praise was directed to recent apostolic movements in which laity are prominent: *Cursillos de Cristiandad, Movimiento Familiar Cristiano, Encuentros de Promocion Juvenil, comunidades eclesiales de base,* and Charismatic Renewal.

Notably, this episcopal letter stressed the vocation and formation of lay ministries and the fresh model of *Escuelas de Ministerios.* These schools of ministry have been established by dioceses during the past decade to prepare lay persons as leaders to serve their diocese and communities. After a core program of Bible study, catechetics, ecclesiology, and social sciences, they are assigned to group ministries according to aptitude and need. After a trial period those who show growth "are then commissioned to serve as lay movement leaders, catechists, lectors, extraordinary ministers of the Eucharist, and small community and study group leaders."

The bishops praised basic ecclesial communities as a great contribution from the church of Latin America, "a ray of hope in dealing with dehumanizing situations which can destroy people and weaken faith." They explained that the *comunidad de base* is "a small community with personal relationships," as "part of a process of integral evangelization . . . in communion with other levels of the Church. The role of the parish, in particular, is to facilitate, coordinate, and multiply the *comunidades eclesiales de base* within its boundaries," among all its members.

The United States bishops concluded then with a new vision for parish life and structure: "The parish should be a community of communities. The ideal *comunidad de base* is a living community of Christians whose active involvement in every aspect of life is nourished by profound commitment to the Gospel."

In order to insure that issuance of their pastoral letter would not be seen as a mere passing event, the bishops tied the pastoral to the long-range "Encuentro process" begun in the early 1970s. The bishops concluded their pastoral by asking "our Hispanic peoples to raise their prophetic voices to us once again, as they did in 1972 and 1977, in a *III Encuentro Nacionel Hispano de Pastoral*. . . . We call for the launching of an Encuentro process, from *comunidades eclesiales de base* and parishes, to dioceses and regions, and to the national level, culminating in a gathering of representatives in Washington, D.C., in August, 1985."

More than 1,100 migrant workers and professionals, homemakers, pastors, and students, designated from 133 dioceses in forty states participated in the third Encuentro. After two years of small group discussions among 25,000 leaders, diocesan representatives brought together concerns and proposals from their local experience. The delegates agreed on four major "prophetic pastoral lines": establishing a "preferential option" for the poor and a "preferential option" for the young; setting the family as the core of pastoral ministry; and pledging promotion of Christian base communities. They also voted "to follow a thrust valuing and promoting woman, recognizing her equality and dignity and her role in the Church."

Archbishop Flores said the Encuentro process "has given all participants a personal experience of being Church. We become owners of the Church. We want to take care of the Church, 'nuestra iglesia.' We want to be responsible for our Church." Cesar Chavez, a delegate who knows about community formation, said, "When people feel it's theirs—the Church, unions, whatever—that's when the dynamic takes place." Archbishop Robert Sanchez of Santa Fe said that until recently Hispanic Catholics "were passive and just listened. Now, we are to be agents, missionaries and constructors of the Church. We no longer belong to the Church; we are the Church."

HISPANICS IN THE 1990S AND BEYOND

As we noted earlier, the United States Bureau of the Census estimates that there will be twenty million Hispanics in the United States by the 1990s. This does not include another two to three million who will be here illegally. It is difficult to obtain precise information on United States Hispanics, partly because a significant portion of the population is migratory. The Northeast Pastoral Center survey estimates that about 85 percent of United States Hispanics are Catholics. National Gallup surveys from 1985 show that 70 percent of Hispanic adults are Catholic. Gallup figures also show that 16 percent of Catholic adults are Hispanic, lower than the percentage implied by the pastoral center's survey.

Differences in sampling techniques and a four percentage point margin of error in each survey account for much of the difference between the Gallup and pastoral center surveys. But what is most important is that both show that the presence of Hispanic Catholics is increasing in both absolute numbers and as a proportion of the Catholic population. This pressure of numbers has spurred the American Catholic church to greater awareness of and response to the needs of Hispanics.

The growing Hispanic presence in the United States church poses both challenges and opportunities. First, the church must understand that Hispanics come from a variety of ethnic and national backgrounds. There are considerable differences, for example, between a Puerto Rican parish in New York, a Cuban parish in Miami, and a Mexican parish in San Antonio. Second, Hispanic Catholics are nowhere near as integrated into parish life as are non-Hispanic Catholics. Third, Hispanic Catholics are the target of intense proselytization campaigns by fundamentalist Christians. Fourth, very few Hispanics are becoming priests, leaving a leadership vacuum in parts of the church. Finally, the pastoral center survey showing low knowledge of Vatican II among Hispanics indicates that the church has a major educational task ahead.

But the growing Hispanic presence also presents several important opportunities for the church. As the churches in the United States and Latin America develop their own "regional" identities, American Hispanics represent a significant bridge in which the American and Hispanic cultures are cross-fertilized. The high and growing percentage of Mexican-Americans could well lead to a higher priority for Mexico in United States foreign policy in the same way that the attachment of American Jews to Israel has emphasized ties between Israel and the United States.

There is also a major irony in the behavior of Hispanic Catholics. On one hand, they rank low in their knowledge of Vatican II. But, on the other hand, they have been highly visible in areas of ministry sparked by the Council. For example, one permanent deacon in four in the United States is Hispanic, and a variety of schools and training programs is increasing the number of Hispanic lay ministers. Hispanics fit very nicely into the growth of lay leadership in American Catholic parishes.

One thing remains clear: As the United States church continues to respond to the challenge of a growing Hispanic population, the major vehicle for responding will be the same one which has greeted previous waves of immigrants—the parish. Developing more information about life in Hispanic parishes and factors which influence the degree of parish involvement by Hispanics is crucial if the church is to do the best possible job of welcoming and integrating Hispanic Catholics into church life.

NOTE

This chapter draws in part on an unpublished report on Hispanic parishes made for the Notre Dame study from its own data bank by Dr. C. Lincoln Johnson, director of the university's Social Science Training and Research Laboratory, with the assistance of Thomas Trozzolo.

A major source for this chapter—not part of the Notre Dame study—is *The Hispanic Catholic in the United States: A Socio-Cultural and Religious Profile* by Robert Gonzalez and Michael LaVelle, foreword by Cardinal John O'Connor, published by the Northeast Pastoral Center for Hispanics, New York (1985).

6. Leaders, Laity, and Decision Making

In the postconciliar American Catholic parish, leadership is a plural noun—both by necessity and design. While the pastor is still central to parish leadership, many other people, most of them laity, share responsibility for the operation and direction of the parish. This has happened by design through efforts to implement the sharing of ministry among ordained and nonordained persons stressed by Vatican II. It has also happened because the declining number of priests, particularly in proportion to the size of the Catholic population, has made it impossible for priests alone to run a parish.

The Notre Dame study examined parish leaders in several ways, including analysis of questionnaires from 35 pastors, 117 paid staff members, and 262 volunteers in the 36-parish sample.

Identifying parish leaders is a particularly difficult task because canon law does not specify which church ministers, other than the pastor, are to be the parish's "leaders." The bishops have encouraged the formation of parish councils and finance committees, but they have not required parishes to have them. Parishes which can afford to do so will appoint and pay people to conduct various programs, but not all parishes can afford hired staff. And simple day-to-day experience offers abundant evidence that filling an important position does not make a person a leader.

David Leege points out that "leadership is fundamentally a matter of reputation. People who are leaders usually get their way; they convince others that something should be done. People who are leaders also get things done; they can be depended on to meet responsibilities. People who do not influence action or who fail to get their tasks done, no matter what their position in an organization, do not maintain their reputation as leaders."

Leege used several techniques to identify the actual leaders in the 36-parish sample. One involved identifying positions that were well located for the exercise of leadership in the parish. These included associate or assistant pastor or pastoral associate; director of liturgy or chair of the liturgy committee (whichever had more power); music director, choir director, or organist; director of religious education; principal of the parish school; chair of the parish council; director of ministry to the sick or aged, or chair of the appropriate committee; and director or chair of the social justice committee.

We asked pastors to supply the names of the people in these positions and to indicate whether each was a volunteer or paid staff. We also asked pastors to name two or more additional paid staff members and four or more volunteers who are "really influential" and "got things done." Pastors added finance committee chairs to the list. Next, the on-site visitors used a technique known as "snowball sampling" by asking those already described as leaders to list other leaders. Finally, we asked pastors and those already on the staff and volunteer lists to name up to ten people who "are more influential than others" and to describe their function in the parish.

These techniques produced a list of 89 of 117 staff members and 202 of 262 volunteers as the principal leaders in the 36-parish sample. Subsequent references in this chapter will be based largely on responses from this group, not from the full sample of staff members and volunteers.

BACKGROUND AND TRAINING OF PARISH LEADERS

The number of leaders within each parish varied widely, from three in a small rural parish to twenty in a large suburban parish. Few leaders were born and raised in the parishes they now serve. Only about one out of every ten pastors and staff members and one out of four volunteers either lived in their current parish, or attended its grade school as a child. The overwhelming majority came to their current parish as adults. They arrived, on the average, about a dozen years ago, only a couple of years earlier than the average parishioner. They did not enter their current parish devoid of organizational expertise, however. Both the average volunteer and staff member had more than a dozen years' experience working in another parish.

In a sense, then, each parish is training not only its own leaders, but also the future leaders of other parishes. Vatican II brought about limited tenure—and therefore greater mobility—for pastors. But the staff and volunteers with whom pastors work are also highly mobile today.

This mobility, however, does not mean that parish staff and volunteers do not develop strong attachments to their parishes. Those reporting the strongest attachments are the volunteers, bringing to mind Thomas Jefferson's observation that loyalty to a country grows in direct proportion to its citizens' participation in self-government. While the volunteer leaders are only slightly more likely than ordinary parishioners to feel the parish meets their spiritual needs, they are quite a bit more likely to feel it meets their social needs. The attachment of paid staff are reasonably high. The weakest attachments are found among pastors and ordinary parishioners.

The parish seems to be an important point of social orientation for volunteer leaders. They are much more likely than pastors and parishioners to say their closest friends are from the parish, with paid staff falling in between. Ironically, although staff members interact a great deal with pastors and other leaders, fewer than half of their closest friends in the parish are fellow staff members. Pastors have the fewest close friends on the parish staff. Apparently paid staff members are no more likely to develop close friendships among the people with whom they work closely than they are with ordinary parishioners. While familiarity in a staff setting does not necessarily breed contempt, it does not yield close friendships.

Parish leaders undertake a great deal of study and reflection in order to better understand their faith and their responsibilities.

Asked to reflect on the last three years, volunteers reported spending an average of eight days on courses, workshops, or seminars
to increase their own religious education or to develop skills related to their parish work. Paid staff had spent an average of eleven
days on the same kind of activity. Over the same three-year period, volunteers had spent an average of nine days and paid staff
an average of fifteen days on retreat. During the past year, volunteers had read an average of eleven articles or books related to
their faith or their parish work, while paid staff had read an average of nineteen such articles or books.

Volunteers have completed more years of formal education than
have ordinary parishioners, and paid staff have completed considerably more years of formal education than have volunteers, with
more than half holding graduate degrees. Paid staff are also more
likely than either volunteers or ordinary parishioners to have attended Catholic schools at all levels. Volunteers are more likely
to attribute their religious training to a Catholic education in general or to workshops. Paid staff, on the other hand, are more likely
to attribute it to a formal degree or credentialed programs.

Volunteer and staff leaders have roughly the same age distribution as adult parishioners. There is a higher proportion of men
among volunteers and of women among paid staff than in the
congregation. But both groups are predominantly female, with
fifty-eight percent of volunteer and staff leaders being female.

Volunteers are more likely than parishioners or paid staff to be
currently married. The staff figure is lower, of course, because of
the presence of women religious. Among those who have ever
married, volunteers have the largest families, parishioners the next
largest, and paid staff the lowest. Volunteers were much more
likely than parishioners to have married a spouse who was raised
a Catholic.

Parish leaders are not only active in a wide variety of parish
organizations, they are also joiners in the outside community. The
average volunteer leader belongs to about twice as many extra-
parish organizations as the ordinary parishioner and has more organizational involvements than either pastors or paid staff. One-

third of the volunteer leaders hold two or more leadership posts simultaneously.

For reasons we can only speculate about, leaders—whether pastors, paid staff, or volunteers—are all more likely than ordinary parishioners to trace their ancestry to Irish roots. Even as leadership moves beyond the priesthood, the American Catholic church remains to a considerable degree "the Irish church."

Volunteer leaders are more likely than ordinary parishioners to be found in white-collar or professional occupations and to have higher incomes than ordinary parishioners, who have slightly higher incomes than paid staff members. By a rough estimate, volunteers contribute three times as much money to the parish as do ordinary parishioners.

According to their reports, volunteers and paid staff attend Mass and receive the Eucharist more frequently than do parishioners, go to Confession and pray more regularly, and are more likely to share their religious beliefs with others. Paid staff are much more likely than either volunteers or parishioners to read the Bible regularly. Both groups of leaders are less likely than parishioners to watch or listen to religious programs; this is probably partly due to the higher percentage of the elderly and retired among ordinary parishioners.

Volunteers have occupied their present posts for an average of six years, paid staff for a little more than five. Two-thirds of the volunteers served in another leadership position within their parish prior to their present one and about 5 percent of these were paid. Among the paid staff, about one-fifth were previously teachers, principals, or pastoral associates in the parish before they moved to their present post. We see, then, that there is also considerable mobility within leadership positions in a parish, as well as from parish to parish.

Curiously, not a very high proportion of the "volunteers"— only 31 percent—actually volunteered for their current responsibilities: 35 percent were recruited by the pastor and 28 percent by other staff members. Among the paid staff, the most common avenues to a parish leadership position were assignment by a bishop or an order, recruitment by the pastor, or personal application—in about equal proportions. A clear lesson for those concerned about parish leadership is that some people are born leaders and some are trained, but they also have to be recruited.

DECISION MAKING IN THE PARISH

Catholic parishes are not only large, they are also organizationally complex: in addition to a pastor and perhaps other full- or part-time priests, parishes may have a parish council, a deacon, a sister, and lay leaders, along with a host of parish organizations. Nearly two-thirds of the parishes studied held staff meetings at least monthly, more often weekly.

About one parish in three uses a planning process to coordinate parish organizational activities. Most of the time, planning is done by the parish clergy and the parish council. In some instances, it is extended to relevant committees or lay organizations. In many instances, either a diocesan representative is involved in the planning process or the diocese operates a program to train pastors and lay leaders in planning. About one in every six parishes will hire an outside consultant to come in, typically for a week, to assist in planning or to help resolve parish conflicts.

We have a more detailed picture of decision making within our 36-parish sample. Within this sample, in those parishes with parish councils, three-quarters meet monthly, a few meet more regularly, and a few meet less often. One-third of the councils consists of elected members only, while all but two of the rest have a combination of elected, appointed, and ex officio members.

The type of business handled by the council varies, often depending on the size of the parish and its staff. In two-thirds of the councils, the pastor presents reports, and in half of them, staff members also report. In all but two of the parishes, the pastor considers the council work to be "planning." However, in only two-thirds of the parishes with councils do staff members consider the council work to be "planning" and in only a little more than half do volunteer leaders see council activity as "planning." Staff and volunteers are somewhat more likely to describe what happens in parish council meetings as "informing" and "reflecting."

This difference in perception about the role of parish councils among pastors, staff, and volunteers may be symptomatic of other perceptual differences in the extent to which they share responsibility. We asked each of the leadership groups, "in general" who normally makes most of the final decisions about parish finances, the parish school, parish organizations, social activities, liturgical practices, and social action programs? The possible responses were "pastor only"; "pastor and council"; "pastor and staff"; "pastor, council, and staff"; "parish council only"; and "other patterns."

What emerged from these questions was a significant perception gap—by and large, pastors reported that they shared decision-making power with others, while staff and volunteer leaders said decision-making power was concentrated in the pastor. The area in which there was the greatest perception of shared responsibility was finances. Pastor and parish council share financial responsibility in more than half of the thirty-six parishes studied. The other extreme is parish organizations. Here the pastor never reports that he makes the final decision when parish organizations are involved, but staff and volunteer leaders believe the pastor remains firmly in control of parish organizations in about one out of five parishes.

Parish social activities also involve a widespread sharing of authority, but the pastor is still heavily involved in two-thirds of the parishes, and, here again, other parish leaders attribute greater control to the pastor than he attributes to himself.

Social action programs, on the other hand, involve greater concentration in the hands of the pastor or the pastor and council. This may reflect the rather limited participation of parishioners in social action programs and the relative newness of parish organizations spefically designed to foster justice and peace in the larger society. At this point in the history of the sample parishes, social action is still more a top-down than a bottom-up activity.

Liturgical practices are even more concentrated, either in the pastor or in the pastor and staff. The parish council is less involved in liturgy than in any other area discussed. Beyond the pastor and staff, a significant number of parishes seem to concentrate power in this area in a liturgy committee.

While 90 percent of volunteer leaders felt they had at least some influence on the pastor, council, and staff, about 40 percent said they wanted more influence. Volunteer leaders felt they were most successful in influencing the pastor and the parish council, somewhat less successful in influencing the paid staff. Those who said they wanted more influence offered a variety of reasons: about one-third referred to clergy control, another third referred to the principle of democracy in any organization, and another third spoke of the need for substantive changes in parish programs or procedural changes in parish governance. Most spoke of the need for widening the group of people who plan, manage, and review in the parish and for the pastor to respect the input of others. Many felt that neither current governance procedures nor parish programs fostered a sense of community in the parish. Several referred to the need for improved liturgy. Others spoke of social programs or reaching out to people who do not feel at home in the parish.

There are a variety of ways leaders feel they can have an impact on a parish. About half of the staff members and a quarter of the volunteers felt they had some control over the parish budget. Roughly the same proportion felt they had authority to staff committees in their domain. And about one-third of the staff and one-sixth of the volunteers felt they acted with the pastor's authority when they acted in their own area of responsibility.

CONFLICT AND CONFLICT RESOLUTION

Another way to examine the sharing of responsibility within the parish is to focus on conflict and conflict resolution. Conflict has become a dirty word in the post–Vatican II church. Pastors and parishioners seem to live in fear of seeing their parishes divided by differences in ideology and priorities. But one should not assume that the presence of conflict in a parish is automatically harmful. There are unproductive conflicts which fester and grow and sometimes destroy a parish, but there are also productive conflicts which help parishes grow. The absence of conflict in some parishes is more likely a sign of rigor mortis than of vitality and community. It's important to recognize that conflicts do, in fact, get resolved. One northwestern parish was the scene of constant conflict between the pastor and the parishioners for almost six years, as parishioners charged their pastor could not—or would not—reconcile competing factions within the parish. The pastor was finally transferred and a new pastor assigned. The parish collection went up by 50 percent in the new pastor's first week. It has stayed at that level ever since, as members of various parish factions welcomed their new priest, who spent a good deal of his time getting to know his parishioners.

Pastors, staff members, and volunteers report some conflict in about three-quarters of the thirty-six sampled parishes. Here, too, we find significant differences in perception. Pastors are about twice as likely as staff and volunteers to say conflict originates within the parish council and that it pits the council against the pastor. Staff members are more likely than others to report that conflict most often occurs between staff and pastor. And volunteers are more likely to see conflict coming from a variety of sources—from a committee member or someone who feels strongly about an issue. The position a person occupies within the parish structure shapes his or her perception of conflict.

Associate or assistant pastors or pastoral associates are the most likely group of leaders to report conflict. They think most of it comes between staff and council, pastor and staff, or pastor and council. The chairs of parish councils are also quite likely to perceive conflict. They view it as occurring within the council, between the pastor and council, within the committee structure, or among parishioners. Principals and directors of religious education are the most likely to view the pastor and staff as the sources of conflict. People responsible for charitable efforts, helping the poor, and visiting the sick report conflict coming from a number of sources. Chairs of liturgy committees and those involved in liturgical music report a great deal of conflict coming from a variety of sources.

Pastors in three-fourths of the parishes reporting conflict are confident that conflict is resolved without one side or the other "winning," but the other leaders are not so sanguine. Staff and volunteers say conflict is talked out or resolved in a satisfactory way in about half the cases. Volunteers are twice as likely and staff members three times as likely to say that if someone "wins," it is the pastor.

One factor in conflict resolution is the way parish leaders feel about one another. We asked the pastors, staff, and volunteers to describe what they liked best and least about the parish staff (including the pastor) and to describe their strong and weak points. Overall, the parish staff is highly regarded. Among volunteers and staff members, positive comments about the staff outnumbered negative comments by three to one. Pastors were even more positive, with a ratio of six to one positive comments.

On the positive side, volunteers were most likely to mention the staff's competence, sensitivity to the needs of parishioners, efforts to improve parish life and programs, and good teamwork. Staff members cited good teamwork, competence, good relationships with the pastor, initiative, and friendliness. Pastors were especially likely to mention competence, good relationships between pastor and staff, and teamwork.

On the negative side, volunteers were most likely to mention bad teamwork and insensitivity to parish needs. Staff members were most likely to mention poor teamwork and poor relations with the pastor. Only poor teamwork received much comment from pastors. All three groups mentioned either the presence of committed volunteer leaders or a shortage of volunteers. Pastors reported having the best relationship with staff members, but staff members themselves reported less satisfying relationships than either pastors or volunteers with other staff members.

Where is dissatisfaction among parish leaders concentrated? The least satisfied staff members are those who serve as either directors of religious education or principals: about 40 percent report poor teamwork and one-third report poor relationships with the pastor. Half of the associate or assistant pastors or pastoral associates report negative comments about the staff. While many feel there is good teamwork, some cite poor relationships with the pastor. The group next most likely to express discontent is parish secretaries, who say they want to see more staff initiative. Liturgical musicians are relatively dissatisfied. Parish council chairs praise staff's competence and sensitivity, but about one-fourth feel there is poor teamwork. But parish council chairs are less likely than other parish leaders to cite unsatisfactory relations with the pastor.

In our parishes, then, pastors and parish council chairs seem to have a high level of respect for each other. Even though they sense the council is at the center of conflict, they share the feeling that most conflicts can be resolved. Some key staff members, however, do not share this respect and optimism. The educators as a group perceive conflict and sometimes complain that the pastor usually wins or that conflict grows. Nevertheless, a high proportion also feel that conflict gets resolved. This paradox can be understood better by looking at male-female relationships in the parish.

WOMEN AND PARISH LEADERSHIP

There is a built-in tension between men and women in parish leadership. One reflection of this is in the fact that the strongest indicators of dissatisfaction with parish decision making is found in the positions disproportionately occupied by women—directors of religious education, organists or choir directors, parish secretaries. This tension is partly the result of a contradiction: while women make up a large majority of parish leaders—58 percent of parish leaders besides the pastor—they are not the most influential leaders. The inner circle of parish leadership is still predominantly male.

Earlier we mentioned that we asked all three leadership groups to name ten of the most influential people in their parish. On the theory that the most influential people would be named first, we examined the gender of the first three people named on each list to get a rough approximation of the "elite" within parish leadership. We excluded the pastors' lists because they were worded in such a way that the pastor would not list himself.

When we examined this new, short list of leaders, we found that about 60 percent of those named were men, despite the fact that 60 percent of those naming parish leaders were themselves women. One reason for the high percentage of men cited as top leaders is the presence of the pastor on most leaders' lists. But even when the pastor is artificially removed from the lists, men are still mentioned more frequently by volunteer leaders, and female leaders are mentioned only slightly more than male leaders by the paid staff.

Despite the overrepresentation of men in top leadership positions, women were no less likely than men to feel they had influence on parish decisions and no more likely to report they wanted more say in how the parish was run. Women volunteers are quite a bit more likely than men volunteers to believe the pastor dominates decisions on school and parish social activities. Women staff members believe the pastor dominates liturgy decisions. Volunteer and staff women responsible for liturgy, social programs, and social activities are the most likely of any group to feel the pastor dominates decision making. All of this hints that women in parish education have developed ways to share authority with the pastor, but women organizing social activities, directing liturgical activities, and leading social programs still feel or are made to feel inferior to the pastor.

Women are less likely than men to perceive conflict among parish leadership. Staff women are the most likely women to report conflict, which they see as coming between pastor and staff. Yet staff women are more likely to say that conflicts get resolved, while volunteer women are more likely to report that conflicts grow deeper. This suggests that staff women—whether through more frequent contact, their own effort, or the pastor's—are better able to communicate their viewpoints than are volunteer women.

To sum up, then, while women have penetrated parish leadership circles in large proportions, they are still not as likely as men to be found in the inner circles. Of course, men had a running start with the male priesthood, and that advantage is not likely to disappear any time soon. It does seem that staff women in some positions are better able than volunteer women and staff women in conflict-centered positions—liturgy, social life, and social action—to cope with male dominance.

THE PARISH AND THE DIOCESE

Parishes do not exist in a vacuum. They operate under the direction of a bishop, who assigns a pastor and possibly other priests, sometimes in collaboration with a regional religious order provincial. Another dimension of parish leadership, then, consists of the relationship of parish leaders to the diocese and the bishop. In order to get at this relationship, we asked pastors, staff, and volunteers, "In general, what do you like best about the operation of your diocese in relationship to this parish? What do you like least?"

First, and not surprisingly, almost half of the parish volunteer leaders had no comment about the diocese because they simply did not know much about it. Diocesan relationships are far more important to pastors and staff members, and they provided more comments on the diocese.

More than one-third of parish volunteers give the diocese positive ratings for moral leadership, good communications, and sensitivity, but a similar proportion gave the diocese negative marks in the same areas. Positive references to support for parish priests, encouragement of the laity, and provision of educational and liturgical resources and training far outweigh the negative references. Quite a few volunteers felt the diocese drains more financial resources than it returns to the parish. About 40 percent of the volunteers commenting on diocesan relations said their parish was somewhat isolated from the diocese either because of its geographical location or because it was staffed by religious order priests, although this isolation was not always viewed as a negative.

Clearly, for volunteer leaders, the parish is a more important frame of reference than the diocese.

Pastors and staff members were considerably more positive in their comments on the diocese. In addition to the positive areas cited by volunteers, pastors praise the diocese for financial support and educational resources. The most negative comments focused on lack of moral leadership and sensitivity. More than half of the pastors in the 36-parish sample complained that the diocese drains off too much in financial resources, takes too much of the pastor's time, and is administratively top-heavy.

The principal bases for the positive ratings of the paid staff are good communications, moral leadership and sensitivity, the provision of resources and training, support for the pastor, and encouragement of the laity. No negative category stands out among the staff.

LEADERSHIP AT WORK

Up until now, we've been looking at what pastors, staff, and volunteers think about leadership. The Notre Dame study's on-site reports also allows us to view leadership at work—good leadership and bad. These observations bring home once again the centrality of the pastor. He sets the tone for all parish activity and makes or breaks a parish. The on-site visits also reveal that successful leadership and unsuccessful leadership are two sides of the same coin—that is, the characteristics of a parish with weak leadership are the reverse of the characteristics of a parish with strong leadership.

For example, in a large suburban parish regarded as successful, the pastor acted as a chief policy officer, broker, and motivator. He followed a model of "enabling" in which his goal was to enable others to do their jobs well. No one doubted that he was in charge, but he was not an autocrat. He delegated considerable authority to his large staff, parish council, and committee chairs. In their respective domains, staff members functioned in the same manner as the pastor. They were held accountable for performance, and one criterion was their ability to involve parishioners in common responsibilities in order to broaden the base of parish leadership. The pastor was well liked by the staff, who regarded him as "quite fair and a real gentleman" even when disagreeing with one decision or another.

Another vital parish, in a city in the mountain states, had adopted a "pluralistic" model of leadership. The congregation was affluent and educated, and the parish tapped into the resources available for expertise—and expertise may be the key word that describes the parish, which seemed to have a ministry to every group in the parish and an outreach program to others. When leaders tried to move into areas outside of their competence, they were blocked. A previous pastor resisted the parish's pluralistic approach, which makes it difficult for a pastor to dominate, but a new pastor has adapted to the parish system.

Other instances of smoothly-functioning, vital parishes reflect some of these same characteristics: a pastor who is decisive, but not dictatorial, and who invites staff, volunteers leaders, and ordinary parishioners to participate in making decisions that will affect the life of the parish. Those decisions may involve liturgy, parish programs, a building drive, parish school, or annual fair—it doesn't matter as long as responsibility is shared. This style of leadership does not guarantee that everyone in the congregation will be happy or that every parish project will go flawlessly; no institution is perfect. But, on the other hand, the on-site reports show that parishes that lack these characteristics have serious problems:

• In one northwestern parish, the pastor usually refused to intervene and often stepped in too late to solve any problems. The decision-making process was fragmented. The staff, parish council, and individual committees operated as separate entities without mutual support or cooperation. Communications channels had broken down and misunderstandings had occurred on who was responsible and accountable for what decisions. The committees had not been held accountable to the parish council and had not coordinated with one another. The pastor had not adequately represented the interests of the staff. His style was almost a laissez-faire approach. He did not want to intervene with decisions made by parish council or staff, but he did not want to be responsible for them either.

- In a southeastern parish, the pastor was nonassertive—he couldn't say no to anyone, didn't lead, and allowed older parishioners to make decisions.
- In a small south Atlantic parish, the pastor was tyrannical. He accused those who criticized his way of running the parish of being "conservatives." (Not all parish tyrants are conservatives.)
- In a south Atlantic parish, the highly popular pastor bypassed parish council to talk with "experts." A parishioner said, "If you have a good man like Father Bob, everything runs so smoothly that you don't hardly need a parish council." But the parish was not building any institutional identity that could continue once the pastor leaves.

There is no doubt about the impact of the pastor's personality on parish life, or as the case may be, the lack of impact. An unassertive or otherwise unavailable pastor often arouses the survival instincts that can be found in many parishes. Faced with a history of high turnover and controversy in pastors, a parish that has to function on its own learns to do just that. The power of the laity in the parish is amazing, with the parish council and committees running everything. The problem, of course, is that the laypeople become so used to running things that they don't allow new pastors much say, and there is constant tension between the pastor and lay leaders.

PASTOR SEPARATION ANXIETY AND TRAUMA

The opposite problem—an overreliance on a dynamic pastor—is more common. One change brought about by Vatican II has been limited tenure for pastors, with the obvious result of more frequent turnover. This, coupled with the natural aging process, has intensified what we call "pastor separation anxiety"—worry about what will happen after Father leaves—and "pastor separation trauma"—what often occurs after Father leaves. The thirty-six parishes surveyed were too small a group to be the basis for a scientific projection to the nineteen thousand United States parishes. Nevertheless, it is highly significant that about one in six of the parishes visited were going through some form of pastor separation anxiety or trauma:

- In a south central church, Father Bob was the cornerstone of the parish. Every parishioner with whom observers spoke praised him highly and noted his highly energetic and motivated personality. They credited him with having had all the new ideas and with having set into motion the strategies for the changes which had taken place. But parishioners also worried about "someday when the bishop takes him away from us . . ." Some parishioners feared that the parish would fall apart when that happened. But most of the parishioners said they would have to hold on to the energy Father Bob had brought to the parish and work harder themselves.

- In a northwestern parish, the pastor was highly popular and totally involved in day-to-day decisions. By diocesan policy, he could stay four more years, but poor health could cut that short. The parish at large seemed not to realize the degree to which the totality of parish life depended upon his direct leadership, but the parish leaders were concerned. They were confident the major programs could be maintained with less direct input from a pastor, but doubted that new ones could be begun.

- In a south Atlantic parish, parishioners were universally concerned about what would happen when the pastor died or retired. He had submitted the required letter of resignation, but had been assured that he could continue as pastor as long as his health permitted. The people saw him as the "heartbeat" of the parish and were fearful of losing him. Some said they would leave the parish if he was replaced by someone more conservative. Others said they would leave if he was succeeded by someone more liberal.

• In a small, rural midwestern parish, many of the parishioners seemed aware of the fact that when the pastor retired he would not be replaced with a resident pastor. This contributed to their desire not to "rock the boat."

• In a midwestern urban parish, the pastor was to retire shortly and there were mixed feelings within the parish about his retirement. He had become so much a part of the very fiber of the parish—had helped make it the community that it was. There was also a sense of fear about the new pastor and what challenges he would offer the parish community. And yet underlying this fear was a sense that what the pastor had brought to the parish would continue to grow and develop in each and every one of the parishioners.

CLIQUES

By stimulating an expansion of lay leadership, Vatican II rejected a pattern of "clericalism" in the church which operated as a double standard—priests, particularly pastors, were more important than other people, particularly when it came to decision making. But as clericalism fades, a new problem emerges—the "clericalism" of credentialed laity and lay cliques which may exercise the same kind of centralized power associated with the old-fashioned pastor. In one southeastern parish, a handful of couples is actually known as "the clique."

• In a south Atlantic parish, one parishioner suggested that there was an unspoken but ever-present undercurrent of tension caused by a tacit caste system based on social status. Therefore, there was an "in-group" and "out-group." The in-group appeared to consist of long-term parishioners who held professional and military titles. They tended to be older, more affluent, and more conservative than the out-group. They seemed to have taken turns holding the elective positions in the traditional and well-established parish organizations such as parish council, sodality, and Holy Name Society, all of which were active forces in parish life. Members of the out-group suspected and resented the fact that these others had a great deal of influence over the pastor's decisions with regard to the spending of money in the parish. The out-group was somewhat disaffected, but was nonetheless vocal. This group was more liberal. One leader had a style which alienated people; the other was more conciliatory.

• In an intermountain parish, a formal network of lay leadership was supplemented by an informal network of friends who were present throughout the leadership structure. This network of friends was known as a "clique" by both the people inside and outside the group. The group did not have firm boundaries, but everyone seemed to be aware of the group.

CONCLUSIONS

There is no doubt that leadership in the post-Vatican II American Catholic parish is very different than leadership before the Council. There is considerably more lay involvement and shared responsibility than in the past. New parish structures, new forms of ministry, new programs have spread throughout the church in all parts of the country and in all communities. Today's parishes are served not just by priests and religious, but by a corps of dedicated, serious, and trained lay staff members and volunteers.

These changes have not come without causing some tensions. Bringing more people into leadership roles does not automatically insure good leadership. There are important perception gaps between pastors and staff, pastors and volunteers, pastors and parish council, staff and volunteers, and so on. Women who move into leadership roles but are still closed out of top leadership positions may become frustrated and angry. New lay leaders can form clerical-style cliques within parishes. And sharing responsibility inevitably brings disagreements, confrontations, and conflicts.

But, as we've noted, conflict does not mean defeat. Conflict and conflict resolution are part of the normal life and growth process of a parish. The post-Vatican II style of parish leadership is still evolving. It will be tested in the years to come as more and more parishes must merge, make do with a part-time pastor, or work under the direction of a parish administrator in order to cope with the growing priest shortage. There may well be more changes to come in parish leadership than in other aspects of parish life.

NOTE

This chapter is based on Report 9 by David Leege, who acknowledges comments and criticisms from Father Philip Murnion of the National Pastoral Life Center in New York; Sister Donna Watzke, O.P., former director of pastoral planning for the Diocese of Fort Wayne–South Bend and currently a psychiatric social worker at Saint Vincent's Stress Center, Indianapolis, IN; and Kathryn O'Hara, an elementary school teacher in South Bend, IN, who has served as chair of a diocesan pastoral council and in several parish leadership positions.

The sections on "Leadership at Work," "Pastor Separation Anxiety and Trauma," and "Cliques" are based on the on-site reports.

7. Liturgy of the Gathered People

In the early 1800s, Catholic liturgy in the United States was noted for its plainness, and church interiors were Spartan in nature, with none of the statues which marked European Catholicism. The statues came later, along with new immigrants from Europe.

The focus of worship was Sunday Mass. In larger churches, there were several Masses each Sunday, beginning very early. In New York, the first Mass was often at 5:30 A.M. Reverential silence was the usual atmosphere for the Mass. Two or three Low Masses were usually followed by a High Mass—with music and singing—at 10:00 or 10:30. Sermons were long, lasting for an hour at High Mass and on special occasions.

Sundays also generally included a period of religious instruction, Confessions, sung Vespers in the afternoon, and Benediction of the Blessed Sacrament—always with a sermon—in the evening. The Eucharistic Host was placed on the monstrance, enthroned on the main altar, and incensed. After prayerful acclamations and hymns, the priest, with great solemnity, blessed the congregation by making the Sign of the Cross over the people with the Sacred Host in the monstrance, while the server rang the altar bell.

Most Catholics received Communion only rarely, perhaps once or twice a year. Once at Easter met the minimal "Easter duty" needed to continue identification as a Catholic. Papal efforts to encourage frequent Communion finally paid off by the 1920s, when a revolution occurred, and reception of Communion became widespread. For example, in Saint Ignatius Church in Portland, Oregon, Communions jumped from 330 in 1919 to 14,400 in 1923, despite the fact that the number of parishioners remained the same.

The Mass, of course, was celebrated in Latin and was dominated by the priest. There was little participation by the people, and the priest even celebrated Mass with his back to the people.

This pattern showed an amazing consistency and stability through the middle of the twentieth century, when "Dialog Mass" was introduced with the use of English missals by the laity. These and related developments of the liturgical movement began in the 1930s. These experiments prepared for the Second Vatican Council which brought a new approach to the liturgy. It set about returning the liturgy to the assembled congregation, making it theirs as the People of God, both as a symbol of unity with God through eternity and as a living gathering of community. The council sought to emphasize the church's communal dimension—the notion of worshiping within a community and having responsibility to the whole community—as distinct from what some have called a "me and Jesus" approach to individualistic spirituality. The new liturgy was designed to help renew the church.

The Council's liturgical reforms included celebrating Mass in the vernacular, the local language, which meant that American Catholics conditioned to hearing the Mass in Latin now heard it in English or their ethnic tongue. They were also asked to participate much more fully in the service—by singing, exchanging a Kiss of Peace to greet their neighbors in the pews, serving as readers and eucharistic ministers, by planning the liturgy, and experimenting with new music and forms. One of these, the "folk Mass" quickly became a hallmark of American Catholicism. An acceptance of pluralism was built into the liturgy of each parish.

The Notre Dame study found that while a number of rough spots remain, the new liturgy has become a reality in American parishes perhaps to a degree few would have anticipated.

THE PROGRESS OF THE MASS

Teams of researchers for the Notre Dame study provided 140 detailed reports on seventy separate Mass celebrations. These observations provide the basis for a walk through the Mass which reveals much about liturgical life in today's parish and the changes emerging since Vatican II.

Catholics form one of four United States church bodies—the others being Lutherans, Episcopalians, and Orthodox—with a strong confessional and liturgical tradition. In liturgical churches, the Sunday service or Mass consists of a liturgy of the Word, built around Bible readings, and a liturgy of the Eucharist. Hymns and chants are integral to these two central stages of the service. Although all four bodies derive from European singing traditions, for a variety of reasons, Catholic Masses in this country were usually Low Masses. At sung Masses, singing and chanting were seldom done by the people but were usually reserved for choir and celebrant.

In contrast, Lutherans and Episcopalians placed special emphasis on full participation by the people in the regular Sunday service. Every twenty to forty years they produced hymnals and service books that shaped parish liturgies. Everyone was expected to sing and chant and speak. The people knew the settings, and the service was easy to follow from the service book or hymnal. Catholics did their singing at devotions and Benediction, but not at Mass. And the Mass, let us recall, was in Latin until 1963.

Vatican II, however, encouraged Catholics to revive the tradition of the sung liturgy. It has come slowly to a people accustomed to taking part in Mass with only spoken responses and, more often, reverential silence. Some complain that the active participation and singing now expected make the Mass "too Protestant." Since, in the past, Catholic teaching did not devote much effort to stimulating the people's direct participation in the Mass, other procedures are now being used to introduce singing, chants, and hymnody and to make the people comfortable with sung participation.

One of the most important of these "remedial" procedures, according to our data, is the pre-service music rehearsal. At a little under one-third of the Sunday Masses we observed, but almost never at Saturday evening Masses, the congregation is asked to rehearse the music to be sung at the Mass. The suburban parishes are most likely to use this procedure and to have it led by a cantor or choir director. It does occur in other settings as well, and in some cases is led by the celebrant. These rehearsals appear to be worth the effort: they tend to lead to increased participation in the service and higher quality music and singing. The same is true when a musical prelude is used to begin the liturgy. These practices may reflect good musical leadership in the parish, but they also serve to signal the people that full sung participation of the Mass is expected.

Perhaps because they involve more preparation and rehearsal, nearly 60 percent of the principal Sunday Masses started late, while the Saturday Mass and secondary Sunday Masses usually started on time. Tardiness at the principal Sunday Mass may also be due to the fact that they were better attended and people were evenly distributed throughout the church. Less than half the secondary Masses filled the church, and people tended to cluster toward the middle and back. Another reason for tardiness at the principal Masses is that they are heavily attended by families, and anyone who has tried to get a family to church knows the difficulties of getting everyone there on time. Also, services often begin late because there is a full schedule of Sunday Masses, particularly in the suburbs. It takes time for the church to empty and refill, and even more time for the parking lot to do the same.

Another Vatican II reform was encouraging the involvement of people besides the priest in formal liturgical roles. In only one of the seventy Masses observed was the celebrating priest assisted by another priest; more often, he was assisted by a deacon. Lay readers (lectors) read at least two of the readings at virtually all of the Sunday Masses but were less likely to be used on Saturday evening. Lay eucharistic ministers are also used at the Masses, but not as commonly as lay readers—they were used at 70 percent of Sunday Masses and 64 percent of Saturday Masses. Although our surveys found that a slightly higher percentage of lay women than lay men served as eucharistic ministers, more men serve on these ordinary Sundays, suggesting that available women may be used as eucharistic ministers less frequently than men. There was a similar pattern with altar servers (acolytes): they were used in almost all Sunday Masses but were absent from one-third of Saturday Masses. Boys and men clearly predominate, but female altar servers were used in about 10 percent of the Masses, more often at secondary Masses.

The Beginnings of the Service

In Lutheran and Episcopal churches and in some Catholic parishes, the service begins with a prelude on one of the principal hymn tunes of the day. The prelude should set the mood for the season of the church year and help parishioners focus their thoughts on the themes found in the readings for the particular Sunday. There was no prelude at 55 percent of the Masses observed; 25 percent used an organist, and the rest used a guitar, flute, choir, or soloist. Some used taped music or taped bells. Even when a prelude was played, it was not necessarily music appropriate for the Sunday.

For more than half the Masses, then, the service did not begin with music but with an entry procession. In only 10 percent of the Masses, typically secondary Masses, was there no procession. In the other 90 percent, the procession varied widely according to the layout of the church and the importance it receives. Processions on "ordinary" Sundays were not very ceremonial. A cross was carried in only one-third of the processions, and lights such as candles were carried in only four of the seventy Masses. There was even less ceremony at Saturday evening Masses. The procession was accompanied by an entry song or hymn at almost all of the Sunday Masses, but only about half of the Saturday Masses.

Practices also varied widely from parish to parish and Mass to Mass on the greeting, the introduction, and the penitential rite. While the Sign of the Cross and the Invocation of the Triune God were rarely omitted, they followed a greeting or opening remarks in more than one-third of the Masses. A greeting such as "good morning" or "good evening" was either substituted for the invocation or added to it at 20 percent of the Masses. At one-third of the Masses, the celebrant went directly from the greeting to the penitential rite. The data indicated that this is associated with poor rapport between parishioners and priest, diminished community awareness, and poor congregational participation.

The Formal Parts of the Opening Rite

The opening penitential rite was only rarely omitted in the seventy Masses observed. The Sacramentary provides three rites. The second is rarely used, and the third is clearly the favorite, especially in Saturday or other secondary Masses. The Kyrie and/or the Gloria were sung at only four of the seventy Masses and, in fact, were sometimes omitted altogether. Typically, they were spoken by the celebrant and the congregation. The Credo was sung at only one Mass. Traditionally, the Kyrie, Gloria, and Credo have been included in every musical setting of the Common, or fixed parts, of the Mass. It is clear that a major shift has evolved in Roman Catholic sung liturgies in this country, a shift not due to any official decision but to popular practices which depart from official directives.

There was more enthusiastic involvement in the opening rites on Sunday than on Saturday. In only half of the Sunday Masses and a third of the Saturday Masses did more than 70 percent of the congregation participate in verbal responses. While missalettes were available at both Saturday and Sunday Masses (about three-quarters of all Masses had them) the congregation is much more likely to make full use of them on Saturday evening than on Sunday morning. Missalettes, then, tend to be associated with lower volume and less enthusiastic participation.

One interesting note: once the Mass begins, fewer than half of those present pray only the prayers and chants of the rite. Four percent seem to ignore the rite and pray only their own prayers. Fifty percent join in the common parts of the liturgy but also add their own prayers.

The Liturgy of the Word

The lectionary, which prescribes which Bible readings will be used on a given Sunday, is in universal use in the parishes observed. In the seventy Masses observed, lay readers usually do the first two readings. In only a few cases did a priest or deacon do those readings. A priest read the Gospel three-fourths of the time, a deacon the rest; one priest chanted the Gospel. The homily was omitted only a few times, and in 80 percent of the Masses it was based more or less on the day's readings.

Different preaching practices are associated with different kinds of parishes. Homilies, except in rural parishes, generally dealt with daily life and reflected an openness to change, rather than an emphasis on traditional doctrine. Homilists in urban parishes were more inclined to preach on matters of private morality, while those in small towns were more likely to address social morality, although there was always a general balance between the two. Rural preachers stuck very close to the reading of the day, were more explanatory in tone, made more use of biblical exegesis, and were more traditional in content. Homilists in suburban parishes were less likely to base their homilies on the readings, were more open to change, were more direct in dealing with current life situations, and were moving, celebratory, and polished in style. Sermons in urban churches were simpler and closer to the readings. Sermons in small town parishes were more likely to emphasize the afterlife but, ironically, more likely to address social rather than personal morality. The average Sunday homily lasted ten to fifteen minutes, while homilies on Saturday tended to be either extremely long or extremely short.

When we relate the kind of homily preached to the overall tone of the celebration, a number of patterns emerge. When sermons were based on the readings, the music was usually appropriate for the day, higher percentages of people joined in the common parts of the Mass, and there were higher levels of engagement and devotion among the laity. When sermons were also moving and celebratory in style, rather than lamenting, priests enjoyed good rapport with their congregation.

Liturgies marked by more emphasis on the sacred than recognition of the congregation were dull. When sermons were open to change and made direct applications to peoples' lives, there was strong congregational singing. On the other hand, sermons characterized by their emphasis on traditional doctrine were more often accompanied by low levels of participation in the Mass.

One striking discovery was that, despite the widely noted emphasis on family life within the parish, very little provision was made in the thirty-six parishes for the needs of children. Their presence was acknowledged only at principal Masses, and then only 20 percent of the time. Some parishes occasionally offered a children's homily or made provision for children's catechesis during the homily.

The Nicene Creed was omitted in 11 percent of the principal and 16 percent of the secondary Masses. It was recited in all but one of the Masses in which it was used. In that case, it was sung.

All but two of the seventy Masses observed had a time for intercessions. In about half the Masses, intercessions were led by a lay reader, cantor, or announcer. This was the case for both principal and secondary Masses. In only a third of the Masses were petitions encouraged beyond those read by the leader. Usually this was done by silent prayer, but occasionally the priest would add other intentions or parishioners would offer their intentions from the congregation.

The Liturgy of the Eucharist

The liturgy of the Eucharist begins with the bringing up of the gifts. Only one Mass in 10 failed to have some kind of offertory procession. In the 90 percent of Masses which had an offertory procession, there was a great variety in the people involved, in the accompaniment, and the gifts. Eighty percent of the time, gifts were brought up by ordinary members of the congregation. Fifty percent of the time, ushers were involved. At Sunday Masses, the procession was accompanied by music—singing, a choir anthem, organ, or guitar—two-thirds of the time. The blessings ("Blessed are you, Lord God . . .") were recited aloud at 30 percent of the Masses. The priest's private prayers were also recited aloud at 10 percent of the Masses, although this is contrary to church rules.

The Eucharistic Prayer was sung at only two Masses, which is not surprising, since it is centuries since this prayer was sung with any regularity. But the preface, the part of the prayer which survived the longest as a sung element, was sung at only six of seventy masses. It seems, then, that the evolving practice is to use music only as a way to get the congregation to join into the people's parts, as opposed to the classic practice in the East and West of setting the entire liturgy to music.

The sung-versus-spoken participation rates involve a curious interplay with hymnals and missalettes. When Eucharastic Acclamations are sung, people perform better if they have hymnbooks than if they have missalettes. When acclamations are spoken, people perform better if they have missalettes. This seems to be due to problems with the way the books are organized. In most hymnbooks, hymns are not grouped by church season or indexed to the lectionary. Some hymnals omit the spoken part of the mass altogether. As a result, parishioners find it difficult to keep their place and follow the Mass. The missalettes are more organized, but few church musicians use the music in them. So when they play different notes than those the parishioners see in front of them, the congregation gets confused and stops singing.

Other factors also influence the level of interest in a congregation during Mass. Congregations get bored when they are expected to sing the whole Mass. They also get bored when they are virtually excluded from the singing because of the dominance of a choir or cantor. People also seem more involved when music comes from an organ than from a guitar. Parishes which have made little progress in implementing Vatican II liturgical reforms had less involved congregations, although the implementation of those reforms does not in itself guarantee involvement. Congregational attentiveness is greatest when there is a strong sense of awareness of a gathered community and when the sense of the sacred it present in the right balance—neither overemphasized nor neglected.

Turning to the Communion rite, it is apparent that the long campaign in favor of frequent Communion has paid off handsomely in American parishes. In 90 percent of the seventy Masses observed, more than three-quarters of the congregation received Communion, with no significant difference from one Mass to another. Where Communion from the cup is concerned, however, the pattern is not so uniform. It was available at only 47 percent of the Masses—44 percent of principal Masses and 51 percent of secondary Masses. Even when the cup was available, a majority of the congregation drank from it in only one-third of the Masses.

Lay people assisted in the distribution of Communion at less than three-quarters of the Masses, with men predominating. At main Masses on Sunday, Communion ministers were used 78 percent of the time, with men assisting at 65 percent and women at 54 percent. Hosts consecrated only at the Mass being celebrated were used in less than 20 percent of the Masses, despite efforts by popes since the eighteenth century to encourage this practice. The general practice seems to be the use of both bread consecrated at the Mass and hosts taken from the tabernacle.

There was congregational singing during the distribution of Communion at three-quarters of the Sunday Masses but only one-third of the Saturday evening Masses, when the accompaniment was as likely to be silence as music played on organ or guitar. It is not clear that the Post-Communion Prayer is universally the conclusion of the Communion rite. Not infrequently, it followed the announcements and immediately preceded the blessings and dismissal. Nearly three-quarters of the Masses concluded with a final hymn or song; the others used instrumental music and a few, silence.

The Quality of the Celebration

The seventy Mass observations provided an opportunity for measuring the overall quality of the celebration. It may come as no surprise that the best quality celebrations were found in the suburbs. Suburban parishes were the most dedicated to implementing Vatican II reforms. They showed the most religious "fervor" at Mass and, along with urban parishes, offered the strongest awareness of a participating community. Urban parishes ranked close behind, although they also had more than their share of uninspiring liturgies, suggesting that liturgy in urban parishes is either very good or very bad. Rural parishes scored surprisingly high on implementing Vatican II reforms—about seven in ten reflected the new liturgy—but they ranked low on religious fervor, awareness of the community, and rapport between priest and congregation.

A major postconciliar change is the increased use of music in the Mass: 90 percent of Sunday Masses and 70 percent of Saturday Masses had some singing. But introducing music is one thing; getting Catholics to sing en masse is another. More than two-thirds of the congregation joined in hymn-singing in only 30 percent of the Masses observed. Participation is quite low when it comes to singing parts of the Mass. The pattern seems to be that the general level of singing the seasonal parts of the Mass is far from impressive. But the congregation does a little better with familiar, repeated texts such as the Sanctus than with texts which change from week to week.

One factor which influences the quality of the celebration is whether a congregation uses a hymnal, songbook, missalette, or individual parish collection of material. Parishes which used missalettes were more likely to show a lack of community awareness during Mass. They were also more likely to have a celebrant who dominated the liturgy but had little rapport with the congregation and who gave dull homilies emphasizing traditional teachings with little relevance to daily life. The heaviest use of missalettes was in rural parishes.

In terms of musical performance, 60 percent of the Masses featured an organist, 60 percent had a choir, one-third had a guitar, and one-quarter had other instruments. A full 40 percent of the Masses featured a cantor, a figure unknown in Catholic liturgy two decades ago. Unlike the cantor in a Jewish service, who functions as a soloist, the job of the cantor in a Catholic service is to engage the congregation in singing the parts of the Mass it is supposed to sing. The cantor sometimes sings a solo, but only for engaging the rest of the congregation. The choir director may double as the cantor, but often the cantor is someone else, yet another lay minister—usually a professional musician—whose role was inspired by Vatican II. The cantor is almost a hallmark of suburban parishes, appearing at four of every five suburban Masses. But the cantor must be very careful not to dominate the singing. We found that congregational singing is the strongest when the cantor leads without dominating. People apparently want leaders, not performers. Similarly, we found that a congregation is much more likely to sing wholeheartedly if it is neither left to do all the singing nor excluded by a choir.

Our observations discovered that singing was stronger when accompanied by an organ than when accompanied by a guitar. This probably has something to do with the positioning of the two instruments and their ability to fill a church with sound. Whe a guitar is used, people at the front sing well, but those at the back do not; there is more uniform participation with an organ. Also, the organist is usually out of sight, while the guitarist is visible and sometimes a distraction.

Perhaps the most significant difference between good and poor congregational singing is the appropriateness of the music to the Mass of the day. Inappropriate music is worse than no music at all. When there was no music, 56 percent of the parishes had most people joining in the common parts of the Mass. But when the music bore little relationship to the Mass of the day, this dropped to eight percent.

The music found in Catholic parishes today consists of hymns and folk songs, with a sprinkling of chants, polyphony, Gospel music, and ethnic hymns. But the folk music which became a symbol of the post-Vatican II Mass leads to very mixed results: it is often associated with very enthusiastic participation, but the participation is usually by a limited part of the congregation. Just as often, a congregation is quite unresponsive to folk music.

The Social Dimension of the Liturgy

The Mass provides an opportunity for Catholics to gather socially before and after the celebration, but such gatherings are far from universal. Only 15 percent of parishes had a formal social gathering before Mass and in only another 40 percent did people gather informally and chat outside the church before Mass. Lingering around after Mass to talk is common in all but suburban parishes. Sixty percent of suburban parishes had no after-Mass gatherings and fewer than one in four served coffee after Mass, as compared to small town parishes where more than one-third served coffee.

Those parishes in which people did gather after Mass were more likely to have a strong sense of community, rites with fuller implementation of the new liturgy, and priests who preached this-worldly rather than other-worldly sermons.

These observations, coupled with other findings from the survey of parishioners, suggest what might be called the "suburban irony." On one hand, as we saw earlier, there is less community in suburban parishes in terms of friendships, conversations, and social life. On the other hand, there is more community in suburban parishes in terms of the celebration of the Mass. These findings are not necessarily contradictory. Each of us is a part of many communities—in our jobs, our neighborhoods, our congregations, our voluntary associations, our friendships. Suburban Catholics seem to have more of these types of communities than those living in other areas. That may be why they are less involved in their parish social communities. But this does not stop them from taking part with enthusiasm in the worship community at Mass.

MASS ATTENDANCE

We noted earlier that only 56 percent of Core Catholics attended their local parish simply because it is their local parish. Today's Catholics are even less concerned about duty when it comes to attending Mass itself—only 6 percent cite the fact that "the Church requires that I attend" as a reason for going to Mass. Another 3 percent cite "habit," and only 2 percent say they attend Mass to please a spouse or parent; 10 percent say they attend to set an example for their children.

Topping the list of reasons for going to Mass (Table 11) were personal preferences—37 percent say, "I enjoy the feeling of meditating and communicating with God," and 28 percent say, "I enjoy taking part in the service itself and experiencing the liturgy."

Table 11. **Core Catholic Attendance at Mass**

REASON FOR ATTENDING MASS	RESPONDENTS GIVING THIS REASON (%)*
I enjoy the feeling of meditating and communicating with God	37
I enjoy taking part in the service itself and experiencing the liturgy	28
I feel a need to receive the Sacrament of Holy Communion	20
I feel a need to hear God's Word	19
I want to set an example for my children	10
The church requires that I attend	6
I enjoy being with other persons in our church	5
Mainly it's habit	3
I want to please or satisfy someone close to me (such as spouse or parent)	2

*Percentages add up to more than 100 percent because respondents gave more than one answer.

Almost 40 percent of the Core Catholics we studied attend services at a parish other than their own some of the time, mostly when they are on vacation or visiting relatives or because of convenience. Only 3 percent say they go to another parish because they prefer the liturgy there. But this figures rises to 11 percent in the suburbs, where freedom of choice is highly valued. Despite a great deal of talk about post-Vatican II Catholics "shopping around" for liturgies, very little of it actually takes place. One major reason for this seems to be the "liturgical smorgasboard" of several types of services offered in so many parishes today. But the main motive for going to one's own neighborhood parish is probably the simple convenience of time and place.

One manifestation of the post-Vatican II "quest for pluralism" has been the emergence of a plurality of liturgical styles within the same parish. American Protestants, who attend the parish church of their choice, have long had a history of liturgical pluralism. But the Catholic church, dominated by the territorial parish, has not. The contemporary parish has responded by serving different communities within the parish with different liturgies. If you don't like the 9:00 Mass, you may love the one at 10:30.

In one midwestern suburban parish, for example, the 7:30 Sunday Mass featured an organ, while the 9:00 Mass featured a guitar. In a small, rural midwestern parish, the Saturday evening Mass was lifeless and without music, while the Sunday morning Mass had music and a much higher level of participation. In a black parish in the south Atlantic region, the Saturday evening Mass featured only an organ and was geared to traditionalist elements in the parish. The 9:00 A.M. Sunday Mass was more polished and had more music, including a flutist. The 11:00 A.M. Mass—by far the best attended of the three—was held in the school hall with ladder-back chairs for celebrant and servers, ruffled curtains, and folk music.

At a middle-class suburban parish in the Northwest, conservatives and those who didn't like to sing or socialize attended the 7:30 or 8:30 Sunday Mass. Those involved in parish renewal programs attended the 10:15 Mass. And the 12:00 or "last chance" Mass was for those who seemed to go merely to fulfill their Mass obligation. At another Northwest suburban parish with a reputation for being "trendy," the Saturday evening and Sunday morning Masses were characterized by staff as "Masses of the living dead," while at 7:00 P.M. Sunday "youth Mass" was well attended.

Overall, Core Catholics attend Mass with great regularity: 72 percent attend weekend Mass every week, another 13 percent attend two or three times a month, and 3 percent atttend once a month. Only 2 percent of Core Catholics say they never attend weekend Mass, while three percent attend once a year, and 8 percent attend several times a year.

Mass attendance varies by age: 50 percent of Core Catholics

under 30 attend Mass weekly. This rises to 61 percent for those 30–39, 72 percent for those 40–49, and 79 percent for those over 50.

While the weekend Mass is the liturgical high point of the week, more than half of Core Catholics attend Mass on a weekday at least once during the year, and 10 percent attend weekly Mass at least once a week; 2 percent report going every day. Four percent go several times a month. Another 3 percent go once a month, 27 percent go several times a year, and 13 percent attend a weekday Mass once a year.

Since the early 1900s when Pope Pius X urged frequent Communion for Catholics, succeeding popes have encouraged the practice. In the post-Vatican II parishes we studied, Catholics do, in fact, receive Communion frequently—80 percent of those who attend Mass also receive Communion. This pattern holds up across age patterns. For example, for Core Catholics under thirty, 50 percent attend Mass weekly and 41 percent receive Communion weekly. Seventy-nine percent of Catholics over fifty attend Mass weekly, and 65 percent receive Communion weekly.

HOMILIES

Core Catholics are ambivalent in their evaluation of homilies. In short, they find them inspiring and interesting, but uninformative and not helpful to the growth of their faith (Table 12).

Table 12. **Core Catholic Opinion on Parish Homilies**

Uninspiring				Inspiring
1	2	3	4	5★
6%	10%	28%	39%	17%
Dull				Interesting
1	2	3	4	5
6%	10%	27%	41%	18%
Uninformative				Informative
1	2	3	4	5
20	37	29	11	4
Doesn't Help				Helps My Faith
1	2	3	4	5
19	33	31	11	6

★Scale of 1 to 5, with 5 the highest ranking

ACCEPTANCE OF LITURGICAL CHANGES

Much has been made of resistance to liturgical changes brought about by Vatican II. Not all changes have been equally well received, but, by and large, most changes have been welcomed by Core Catholics (Table 13).

Table 13. **Core Catholic Opinion on Liturgical Changes**

CHANGE	WISH IT WERE OMITTED (%)	DON'T MIND (%)	HAPPY IT'S ADDED (%)	OUR PARISH DOESN'T DO (%)
Hymn singing by congregation	4	27	67	2
Exchanging a sign of peace	12	24	61	3
Communion from the cup	15	32	35	17
Communion in the hand	10	30	59	1
Lay readers	6	34	60	1
Silence after reading and the homily	6	37	41	16
Lay men Communion ministers	15	37	44	4
Women Communion ministers	18	31	38	13

Interpretation of these findings depends partly upon whether you view the "I don't mind" response as a glass that's half full or a glass that's half empty. If you view it as indifference, the responses seem less enthusiastic than if you view it as passive acceptance. It's more instructive to look at the ratio of "I'm happy it has been added" to "I wish it were omitted"—we call this the "happy/unhappy" ratio.

With this perspective, the greatest resistance is to women communion ministers. Even here, however, the proportion happy with the change was twice as large as the proportion unhappy with it. The fairly large percentage of parishes which do not have women communion ministers—13 percent—is a further indication of resistance. Given the degree of resistance, the 31 percent who say they don't mind women communion ministers are significant simply because they do not actively oppose the change. There is greater acceptance of men communion ministers.

Two parts of the Notre Dame study provided a discrepancy on the use of lay communion ministers and the use of the cup for Communion. Only 4 percent of parishioners said their parish did not have lay communion ministers, but there were no such ministers in 23 percent of the Masses observed. Similarly, only 18 percent of parishioners said their parish did not offer Communion from the cup, but it was not offered at 52 percent of the Masses observed. These discrepancies suggest that the liturgical pluralism noted above extends to including changes at some Masses but not at others within the same parish.

Communion from the cup, in fact, has the second lowest happy/unhappy ratio, with barely twice as many Core Catholics happy with the change as unhappy. Study observers found that more than 70 percent of the congregation took Communion from the cup in only 17 percent of the Masses at which it was offered. This suggests that the church has not successfully explained the reasons for offering Communion in the cup. It might also, of course, indicate a reluctance to share a common cup for fear of communicable disease.

But if there is resistance to Communion from the cup, Communion in the hand is widespread and quite popular. Barely one percent of parishioners said their parish did not offer the practice, and the number of those happy with the change is six times larger than the number unhappy with it. It was not until the mid-seventies that the United States bishops overcame internal opposition and voted to allow Communion in the hand. But their people were clearly ready for the change.

The remaining changes are quite popular, including the Sign of Peace or Kiss of Peace which provoked considerable opposition when it was first introduced. It is now all but universally offered and has a happy/unhappy ratio of better than 5:1. Lay readers are highly popular, and silence after readings and the homily is popular when used.

The most popular post-Vatican II change is the addition of hymn singing by the congregation. It, too, is almost universally available in the parishes we sampled and has a happy/unhappy ratio of better than 16:1. Core Catholics seem to take their new-found singing seriously. However, while extremely popular, it is also the element of parish celebration seen as most in need of improvement—one Core Catholic in three sees a need for improved singing, slightly more than the 27 percent who see a need for improved music in general at Mass. Satisfaction with other elements of the Mass—readings, prayer, and ritual—are considerably higher—in fact, remarkably high (Table 14).

Table 14. Core Catholic Opinion on the Mass

Aspect	Generally Unsatisfactory	Could Be Improved	Generally Satisfactory
Music	7★	27	66
Readings	3	13	84
Singing	7	33	60
Prayers	3	15	83
Ritual	4	14	82

★Percentage of respondents

Two factors seem related to increased satisfaction with a parish's liturgy—the degree of planning involved and the degree of implementation of Vatican II reforms.

Liturgists hold out an ideal for collaborative planning that includes development of homily themes through reflection on the readings of the day and application of them to concrete situations locally and in the world at large; similar selection of music appropriate to the mood and theme of the day; selection from among appropriate ritual options; the composition of introductions, prayers, commentaries, or bulletin notices; and, finally, continuous nurturance of technical competence, theological understanding, and spiritual motivation.

Like most ideals, this one has not been realized, at least not in the thirty-six observed parishes. But we used that ideal to divide the parishes into four categories in terms of planning—strong, moderate, weak, and none. We then divided the thirty-six parishes into four groups ranking from highest to lowest satisfaction levels based on responses to the above questions on satisfaction with different aspects of the Mass.

We found that of the nine most satisfied parishes, four had strong liturgy planning, two had moderate planning, and three had weak planning. Of the nine least satisfied parishes, three had strong liturgy planning, but six had weak planning.

This suggests some positive relationship between planning and parish satisfaction with liturgy. But planning does not necessarily insure satisfaction. For example, some parishes have weak planning, but high satisfaction. In two such instances, parishes were living off the legacy of strong leadership from a previous pastor. Other parishes have strong planning, but low satisfaction because of other internal splits, such as between "traditionalists" and "progressives."

Another way of looking at satisfaction is by relating it to the degree of Vatican II reforms present in the liturgy. We examined thirty-six Masses at the nine most and nine least satisfied parishes and related them to postconciliar liturgical celebration, based on the observers' evaluations, with "high consistency" indicating the most consistency with Vatican II reforms (Table 15).

Table 15. **Liturgical Reforms Related to Parish Satisfaction**

CONSISTENCY WITH VATICAN II REFORMS	MASSES AT THE MOST-SATISFIED PARISHES	MASSES AT THE LEAST-SATISFIED PARISHES
High consistency	9	3
Medium consistency	3	1
Neutral	2	2

Consistency with Vatican II Reforms	Masses at the Most-satisfied Parishes	Masses at the Least-satisfied Parishes
Medium inconsistency	3	1
High inconsistency	1	12

A clear pattern emerges. The parishes in which people are the least satisfied with their liturgies are the ones which do not reflect Vatican II reforms. The parishes in which people are most satisfied with their liturgies are those which do reflect the post-Vatican II liturgy.

All in all, findings on the relationship of planning and degree of implementation of Vatican II reforms indicate that liturgy is more a barometer of parish health than the primary cause of high or low morale. While the liturgy provides an important focus for the parish community's sense of identity, the liturgy alone cannot provide that identity. Vatican II taught that the liturgy is the "source and summit" of the Christian life, but it also recognized that there is more to the life of the church than liturgy. The liturgy does not exist as an abstract ideal but as a concrete reality whose shape and vigor are derived, not merely from the official books, but from the histories, hopes, experiences, and relationships of the people who gather to celebrate it in particular times and particular circumstances. In a sense, the Notre Dame study confirms what liturgists have held to be fundamental—liturgy often mirrors what is happening in the parish community.

CONCLUSIONS

The new liturgy, the post-Vatican II liturgy, is not a full reality in every Mass in every Catholic parish in the United States. Some of the Council's reforms—such as hymn singing and the Kiss of Peace—are much more popular than others, such as Communion from the cup or women eucharistic ministers. But in less than a generation, the new liturgy has become both the ideal and the standard in American parishes. American Catholics have accepted and endorsed the new liturgy and they take it seriously. They are less likely than before the Council to participate out of obligation alone and far more likely to participate because they want to. And they want to because they find meaning in the Mass and feel a part of it.

The Notre Dame study also reveals some problems with the implementation of the new liturgy. One involves the risk of losing a sense of ritual prayer. Christian liturgy is and always has been— in principle, at least—the prayer of the community. It is also ritual prayer, characterized by repetition of the same acts, rehearsing of the same words, celebration of the same symbols, and singing of the same chants. Community celebrations tend to become ritualized, for without repetition and familiarity communal participation would be difficult, if not impossible, especially in preliterate cultures. Thus, the Christian liturgy developed certain recognizable features and familiar forms in different church communities, and different rites of East and West evolved. Liturgy is characteristically traditional, though not necessarily uniform from one church to the next. Over the centuries, of course, these diverse traditions were developed, borrowed, pruned, and reformed because liturgy is not static.

The "fixing" of the liturgy, however, was never absolute. There was, for example, a wide range of chants available for Sundays and holy days. There were processions and litanies for specific days. There were occasional offices and feast days. The church calendar, then, provided a rich repertoire of variable elements suited to particular occasions built around unchanging elements, such as the Canon of the Mass. The keepers of the tradition always knew how the structure was to be observed and how the variable elements were to be used. The pre-Vatican II Roman Catholic liturgy was frequently sloppy and slapdash, but it was usually celebrated whole and intact.

In the postconciliar period, the taken-for-grantedness of traditional ritual forms seems to be declining. In part, this may be the result of the very process of liturgical reform itself; if something could be changed, than anything could be questioned. Or it may be symptomatic of the American way of life which places a premium on innovation.

Whatever the reason, it does not appear from the observers' reports that those responsible for liturgy in United States Catholic parishes think of the Sunday liturgy as the rehearsal of old, familiar rites. The legalism which used to protect the Mass to some extent from idiosyncratic changes seems largely to have waned. In its place, enthusiasm and goodwill have to substitute for a sense of the rite. As a result, important elements of the Mass structure are sometimes omitted or distorted by misunderstanding. Often the freedom given to the community to plan and adapt the liturgy results in poor or inappropriate selection of prayers, readings, and, especially, music. Sometimes the people responsible for planning or celebrating the liturgy fail to communicate adequately with each other or simply act without paying attention to each other.

Such lapses would be more rare if those concerned had had the opportunity to reflect on liturgy as ritual. Too often liturgy lapses into rote performance or gusts of enthusiasm, neither informed by a reverent respect for the tradition or by a grasp of the nature of the liturgical act. At its best, liturgy is the prayer of a living community united in one body before God so that their daily lives come to reflect that new identity. When that happens, the congregation feels in communion with the whole Church throughout the world and the generations who have gone before them. They become part of something much larger than themselves.

Another problem in implementing the new liturgy is an example of the "law of unintended consequences." One major liturgical reform stemming from Vatican II was allowing Catholics to fulfill their Sunday Mass obligation by attending Saturday evening services. It gave individuals and families some flexibility and was expected to increase participation. But, to be blunt, if you want to attend a Catholic Mass that is well planned, has vibrant music, and is well attended by people who want to share the liturgical life of their church—don't go on a Saturday evening.

A pattern that emerged with overwhelming regularity in the analysis of weekend services was that the Saturday evening Mass has become a ghetto where uninterested priests lead dull services for bored people. We don't know whether this is the case because those who attend Saturday evening Mass do so simply to meet their Mass obligation and are not interested in participating or because priests and liturgical planners treat the Saturday evening service as though it were not the "real Mass." It may well be a little bit of both. But whatever the reason, Saturday evening services represent the desert of post-Vatican II liturgical life.

The Notre Dame study also found some practical steps which seem to be working in parishes today to increase participation in and satisfaction with the Mass. Some require a certain amount of resources and sophistication, but others are easily within reach of every parish in the country.

1. *Planning.* Good planning—which requires collaboration among pastor, musicians, and liturgists—by itself does not assure good liturgy, but it certainly increases the odds that liturgy will inspire more widespread participation and higher levels of satisfaction.

2. *Rehearsal.* Rehearsing before Mass the hymans to be sung during Mass increases the spirit of participation.

3. *Greeting.* Some liturgical purists may wince at the notion of opening a Mass with "good morning" or "good evening," but a simple greeting seems conducive to a rapport between priest and congregation and invites participation.

4. *Awareness of Community.* Participation increases when a priest establishes a rapport with his congregation and an awareness of a sense of community, a gathering of the People of God.

5. *Homily.* Homilies which are open and not rigidly traditional in approach, which are moving and celebratory in style, which address the people as a congregation, and which relate the readings of the day to the daily lives of parishioners encourage participation in the liturgy.

6. *Music.* When music is appropriate to the Mass of the day, when hymnals are used, and when there is a balance between congregational and solo singing, participation increases.
7. *Sacred/Secular Balance.* When a Mass reflects a balance between the sacred—an awareness of mystery—and the secular—awareness of the concrete life situations of the congregation—participation increases.
8. *Gathering after Mass.* A social gathering after Mass seems to increase the sense of community within the parish; this sense of community in turn increases participation in the liturgy—there can be something sacramental in a cup of coffee and a chat.

All of the steps which increase satisfaction with liturgy do so because they increase participation. Before Vatican II, American Catholics were silent observers at their Masses, religious celebrations conducted by others. Today, they are not observers but participants in a liturgy which celebrates their role in the community of the People of God.

NOTE

This chapter is based on Reports 5 and 6 by Mark Searle and David Leege. The report authors acknowledge comments and criticisms from Sister Kathleen Hughes of the Catholic Theological Union, University of Chicago; Father Robert Schmitz of the Cincinnati Archdiocesan Office of Planning and Research; and Sister Eleanor Bernstein of the Center for Pastoral Liturgy, University of Notre Dame.

Additional material in this chapter comes from the parishioner survey and on-site reports.

8. Devotions Past and Present

From the middle of the nineteenth century through the Second Vatican Council, Catholic devotions—a variety of processions, celebrations, and prayers to a variety of saints, which emerged in the United States with the influx of European immigrants—represented one of the most colorful aspects of church life.

Many of these were devotions to the Blessed Virgin Mary. One form of Marian devotion was the May devotions, which included evening services honoring Mary several times a week, culminating the month in a procession and the "crowning" of a statue of Mary, usually outdoors. The most distinct form of Catholic devotion to emerge was the praying of the Rosary honoring Mary. The devotion consists of fingering a string of beads made up of five sets each of one large and ten smaller beads. Each set is called a "decade," with the large bead representing an "Our Father" and the small beads a "Hail Mary." The usual devotion is five decades while meditating on the joyous, sorrowful, or glorious aspects of the lives of Jesus and Mary. Catholics prayed the Rosary both in private and in public services. Another popular devotion was the Novena, nine consecutive evenings of prayer and devotion for a special occasion or intention.

Catholics were not allowed to eat meat on Fridays and meat was permitted only on Monday, Tuesday, and Thursday between the First Sunday of Lent and Palm Sunday. A popular Lenten devotion was saying the Stations of the Cross, meditations on fourteen scenes from Christ's condemnation to death through his burial in the tomb, which were displayed on the church's interior walls.

These devotions added to a sense of Catholic spirituality and related various ethnic traditions to the universal Church. But many Catholics today regard these devotions as outmoded relics from the church's past. The Notre Dame study makes clear that there has been a significant shift in Catholic devotional patterns since Vatican II. We have no hard data with which to compare the new findings. But no doubt a significant decrease has taken place in the observance of pre-Vatican II devotions and the emergence of a new style of devotion since the Council (see Table 16).

Table 16. **Frequency of Core Catholic Devotions and Confession**

DEVOTION	NEVER (%)	ONCE A YEAR (%)	SEVERAL TIMES A YEAR (%)	AT LEAST MONTHLY (%)	AT LEAST WEEKLY (%)
Benediction	53	28	15	2	2
Stations of the Cross	44	35	17	2	2
Public Rosary	61	18	15	3	3
Novena	76	14	6	1	2
Communal penance	50	29	18	2	1
Confession	26	35	33	6	1

The study showed that while men and women are equally likely to attend Benediction, women—and particularly older women—are far more likely to be involved in Novenas, Stations, and public praying of the Rosary. The major differences occur by age groups. Well over half and sometimes as many as 85 percent of young Catholics rarely or never participate in Stations, Novenas, public Rosaries or Benedictions. Participation increases with age, but the major increase is usually around age sixty. These findings are not conclusive, but they strongly suggest that pre-Vatican II devotions have simply not persisted among post-Vatican II Catholics. It is still possible, however, that more young Catholics will adopt some of these practices as they grow older.

CONFESSION AND COMMUNAL PENANCE

Confession and communal penance services require special attention. In recent years, Pope John Paul II and the American bishops have sought to focus more attention on private confession. Weekly confession before Communion is common in some Catholic countries, and some say it is the defining characteristic of Catholics in Poland, where it is said long lines at Confession are rivaled only by the long lines at food stores. But church leaders have expressed widespread concern about a declining frequency of private Confession in the United States.

Among Core Catholics in our sample, 26 percent never go to Confession—compared to only 6 percent who never or rarely attend Mass and 11 percent who never or rarely receive Communion. Another 35 percent go to Confession once a year; 33 percent go several times a year, with 6 percent going once a month and 1 percent going more frequently than that. Volunteer leaders are somewhat more likely to go to Confession. But even among this group 15 percent never go to Confession.

The use of both private Confession and communal penance is associated with age. Catholics over sixty are far more likely to go to Confession than are younger Catholics. Three-quarters of Core Catholics under thirty go to Confession once a year or less: 38 percent never go to Confession and another 37 percent go once a year; 20 percent go several times a year; and only 5 percent go once a month or more.

While fewer Core Catholics are going to Confession and going less often, Confession continues to be readily available in the parishes. Of the thirty-six parishes visited, thirty-two had a weekly Confession schedule ranging from fifteen minutes to six hours. All thirty-six pointed to the availability of unscheduled Confession outside of regular hours, and priests heard a handful to a dozen of these each week. Several pastors said that if regular Confessions are to be increased, they will have to have more priests or reorder parish priorities.

Nine of the parishes have the traditional Confession which encourages anonymity, eleven have the modern confessional (or reconciliation room) which encourages face-to-face exchange. Fourteen parishes have both forms. Parishes without confessionals in the church itself use the rectory office or some other location as the reconciliation room. Even when traditional confessionals are the only facilities visible, pastors report hearing Confessions on a face-to-face basis in many settings outside visits to the sick. Furthermore, the physical presence of a confessional does not mean that the confessional is where most Confessions are heard. In five parishes, the confessional was either unused or used for storage, and Confessions were heard in face-to-face settings elsewhere. There seems to be movement away from a "checklist" form of Confession in favor of longer personal discussions of guilt and healing.

There seems to be considerable confusion about communal penance services, which have become common within United States parishes only in the past decade. A sizeable portion of Core Catholics said communal penance was not available in their parish. A few pastors replied that communal penance violated church law, presumably because they believed such services involved general absolution for parishioners who had not confessed privately. Whatever the reason, 50 percent of Core Catholics had never participated in a communal penance service that they had recognized as such, 29 percent had done so about once a year, 18 percent several times a year, and 3 percent more regularly than that.

Communal penance rites may have replaced private Confession for only a small portion of Core Catholics. Most commonly, people rely on both or practice private Confession alone. Among Core Catholics, 18 percent neither go to Confession or take part in communal penance rites, 7 percent participate in communal penance rites but do not go to private Confession, 31 percent go to private Confession but never participate in communal penance rites, and 43 percent do both. Contrary to fears about younger Catholics, one age group is no more likely than another to replace Confession with communal penance. Furthermore, the more often a person participates in communal penance rites, the more likely he or she is to go to private Confession. At the same time, the more often a person goes to private Confession, the more likely he or she is to take part in communal penance rites.

Communal penance is available to a higher degree than parishioners realize. Within the thirty-six parishes visited by research teams for the Notre Dame study, all but five offered Rite II at least during Lent and often during Advent. Several parishes offered it more often, and several offered it weekly. In this rite, the entire congregation generally participates in a common process of examination of conscience. Then, priests are stationed at several places around the church to hear private Confession and offer the Sacrament of Reconciliation.

Nine of the parishes have also used Rite III, which involves general absolution; three of the parishes use it exclusively. Pastors are expected to report the use of general absolution to their bishops because it is to be used only in emergency situations when it is impossible to hear private Confessions and extend the Sacrament of Reconciliation over a large group of Catholics.

The study findings do suggest that in those few parishes which practice general absolution, a higher percentage of people never go to private Confession. In the parishes which use both Rite II and Rite III, between 21 and 31 percent of the members never go to Confession. In the parishes which use only Rite III, between 41 and 49 percent never go to private Confession. But this is not conclusive in that it does not tell us which came first, the chicken or the egg—some argue that the availability of general absolution is the reason some people never go to private Confession, while others argue that communal Confession with general absolution is a pastoral means for dealing with people who otherwise would never confess. Our findings cannot settle that debate. Despite concern about the impact of communal penance services, however, Mark Searle and David Leege conclude that "where the rites are used in conjunction with confession, there is little reason to be alarmed that they will become the occasion of 'cheap grace.' "

It is clear that frequent Confession is no longer part of the religious consciousness of Core Catholics. But Confession remains a part of their Catholic identity for three-quarters of Core Catholics.

When it comes to other forms of devotional activity and spirituality, Core Catholics are much more comfortable with and likely to turn to private prayer than Bible reading or collective prayer (Table 17).

Table 17. **Frequency of Core Catholic Devotional Activities**

ACTIVITY	NEVER (%)	ONCE A YEAR (%)	SEVERAL TIMES A YEAR (%)	AT LEAST MONTHLY (%)	AT LEAST WEEKLY (%)
Read or study the Bible on your own	33	20	21	11	16
Read or study the Bible with friends or as part of a study group	73	8	7	5	8
Say grace before meals	8	4	21	8	59
Listen to a religious program on the radio	60	9	12	6	13
Watch a religious program on television	52	14	20	6	10
Pray with friends or members of your family or household, other than grace	44	11	17	7	14
Pray privately	3	1	6	6	80
Fast, or abstain from meat on certain days	16	14	48	7	15
Share your religious beliefs with other Catholics who have similar beliefs	15	10	32	22	22
Share with Catholics with different beliefs	26	16	31	15	12
Share with non-Catholics with similar beliefs	25	18	32	15	10
Share with non-Catholics with different beliefs	31	21	29	12	7

American Catholics continue to be more likely than American Protestants to practice their religion privately outside of Mass. We see, for example, that while 80 percent of Core Catholics said they pray privately at least once a week—including 61 percent who do so daily—only 14 percent pray with others at least weekly. Similarly, Bible study continues to be a low priority for Core Catholics, with almost three in four reading the Bible no more than several times a year. This makes the one in six who read the Bible at least weekly a fairly striking figure.

The high percentage of Catholics saying grace before meals at least weekly—59 percent, including 42 percent who say grace daily—is something of a surprise and indicates a retention of a devotional sense of thanks and praise on a frequent basis. Saying grace with members of their family is the most group-oriented form of devotion most Core Catholics engage in outside of Mass.

On another meal-related devotion—fasting—we see that, in the wake of the end of the formal ban on eating meat on Friday after the Council, only 15 percent of Core Catholics say they fast weekly and only another 7 percent fast monthly. The United States bishops probably did not expect fasting to drop to that level. But, on the other hand, only one in six Core Catholics never fasts—about half fast several times a year, presumably during Lent and at other key points in the church year. The practice of fasting has not disappeared; it has become a form of devotion reserved for special occasions.

Core Catholics are not major fans of religious broadcasters, the radio preachers and "televangelists" who have received such publicity in the past decade. When they do listen to or watch such programs, it is usually a local program or a Sunday Mass. Six percent report watching a Billy Graham Crusade, and 5 percent report watching "The 700 Club," which has a talk-show format.

Core Catholics are most likely to discuss their religious beliefs with other Catholics with similar beliefs than with anyone else: 44 percent talk about their faith with fellow Catholics with similar beliefs at least once a month, while only 19 percent discuss their faith with non-Catholics with different beliefs during the same period. But Core Catholics are as likely to discuss their faith with non-Catholics holding similar religious views—25 percent at least once a month—as they are to discuss it with Catholics with differing view—27 percent at least once a month.

Overall, Sunday Mass remains the most fulfilling religious practice for a plurality of Core Catholics—43 percent cite it as the most fulfilling, followed by 29 percent who cite private prayer, and 8 percent who cite receiving Communion.

THE OBJECT AND CONTENT OF PRAYER

As with their public religious life, Core Catholics differ greatly among one another in their private prayer lives—members of the same parish may have very different prayer styles, and different parishes may emphasize different types of devotions. Historically, certain devotions—such as to the Blessed Mother, the Sacred Heart, or a saint—are associated with various ethnic groups or religious communities. The Second Vatican Council placed renewed emphasis on Christ as the center of the church and of prayer.

The Notre Dame study asked parishioners to describe their prayer life—to whom do you usually pray (Table 18), and what do you pray about? (Most parishioners gave at least two answers, so totals add up to well over 100 percent.)

Table 18. **Focus of Prayer Among Core Catholics**

PERSON	RESPONDENTS MENTIONING THIS PERSON (%)
Jesus	63
Mary	46
Father, Lord	28
Holy Spirit	15
St. Jude	6
St. Joseph	4
St. Anthony	3
St. Theresa	2
Sacred Heart	1

PERSON	RESPONDENTS MENTIONING THIS PERSON (%)
Other (includes saints with less than 1% and unspecified "saints")	15

These findings indicate a dramatic change in the prayer life of American Catholics. Jesus is clearly the primary focus of prayer for parish-connected Catholics in the postconciliar church. Not only is he the most mentioned, he is also the first mentioned by more than half of respondents. The other members of the Trinity—the Father and the Holy Spirit—are substantially behind Jesus and trail Mary. Typically, Mary is the second person to whom parish-connected Catholics pray. Saints remain important in the private devotional life of parish-connected Catholics: as many Core Catholics cite prayer to a saint as cite prayer to God the Father.

But some very important distinctions lie behind these patterns. One question which comes to mind is what impact the Second Vatican Council's emphasis on Christ as the center of church life has had. David Leege examined the relationship of age to style of prayer. He classified Core Catholics in four ways: (1) by the extent to which their prayer is directed exclusively to a member of the Trinity; (2) whether it is directed to a member of the Godhead and Mary; (3) whether it includes the Godhead, Mary, and saints; and (4) whether prayer is addressed only to Mary and the saints (Table 19).

Table 19. **Focus of Prayer Among Core Catholics, by Age**

OBJECT OF PRAYER	RESPONDENTS UNDER 40 (%)	RESPONDENTS OVER 40 (%)
Only Godhead	57	34
Godhead, Mary	22	29
Godhead, Mary, saints	17	28
Only Mary, saints	4	8

These findings reveal clear patterns along age lines. Younger parish-connected Catholics are far more likely to address the Father, Son, and Holy Spirit alone; fewer than half pray to Mary or a saint at all. Older parish-connected Catholics are still likely to pray to a member of the Godhead but also to Mary and the saints.

There were also wide regional differences in style of prayer life. To look at the extremes, all fourteen parishes with more than forty-five percent of their members praying exclusively to a member of the Trinity are located south of the Mason-Dixon line or west of the Mississippi River. On the other hand, seven of the nine parishes where 10 percent of the members prayed only to Mary and the saints are in the northeast or upper Midwest, typically in recognizably ethnic parishes.

To some extent, age interacts with these regional differences, but age alone does not tell the whole story. There seems to be a parish "prayer culture" that is shared by old and young alike. For example, in parishes where very high proportions of older women pray to Mary and the saints, higher than average proportions of younger women also pray to Mary and the saints. Where prayer exclusively to a member of the Trinity is very popular, it is also found more than the average among the older people.

Leege says, "We suspect there is a process of assimilation operating behind these devotional patterns. In some states or enclaves where Catholics predominate, it seems quite natural to involve Mary or the saints in one's devotional life. In other states or locales where Protestants are predominant, prayer life involving only members of the Trinity seems more natural. In future years, it will be interesting to see whether the continuing assimilation of Catholics to the culture around them will affect private devotion, or whether the migration of large numbers of Catholics to parts of the country where they have not typically lived in large numbers will transplant the devotional styles of the older enclaves."

We now know to whom Core Catholics pray. But what do they pray about? Usually they pray to express thanks, to seek guidance in their personal lives, and to ask for good health for themselves and their families. Nineteen percent in our study pray to give thanks; 12 percent ask for guidance; another 8 percent pray "to be a good person"; 9 percent pray for their own health and another 7 percent pray for their family's health. Nine percent mention "emotions" in their prayer, and 6 percent mention family emotions. Four percent pray for forgiveness, and four percent pray for peace.

CORE CATHOLICS AND GOD

There is a great deal of confusion and diversity among Core Catholics as to precisely how God relates to the world and to their salvation. In a sense, this should not be surprising, given the lack of theological education of most lay people and the sense of mystery surrounding God.

Table 20. **Core Catholic Opinion on God's Relationship to the World**

VIEW	RESPONDENTS VOICING THIS VIEW (%)
God and the world are one	15
The world is part of God, but God is greater and larger than the world	39
Human beings are part of God	24
God sets the world in motion but does not play an active role in the world	3
God transcends the world, entering the world infrequently	1
God transcends the world but is actively involved in the world	18

The diversity of answers in Table 20 also suggests that no one description is sufficient—several answers, perhaps the second, third, and sixth, might well apply. The same kind of confusion and diversity of opinion can be found in response to questions about the relationship of Christ, the church, and salvation (Table

21). Here, for example, we might suspect that Cardinal Joseph Ratzinger, head of the Vatican's doctrinal congregation, would choose the third response, the response chosen by one-fifth of Core Catholics—while almost half give a more direct-to-Jesus reply.

Table 21. **Core Catholic Opinion on Christ, the Church, and Salvation**

VIEW	RESPONDENTS VOICING THIS VIEW (%)
God has sent his son, Jesus, to save us, and since he has completed that, each of us individually can approach God directly	23
God has sent his son, Jesus, to save us, and since he has done that and continues to do it, each of us individually can approach God through Jesus	25
God has sent his son, Jesus, who continues to live in the church. As a result, the church teaches and sanctifies us for God	21
Since the church is Christ's body and since we, its members, are the church, together we approach God directly	21
Jesus was a great man, but not really God. Jesus showed us how to live our lives	1

Catholics vary also on the role they see for the Holy Spirit: 43 percent say the Spirit's role is "to guide each of us (if we pray)"; 37 percent say "to unite us to Christ"; 10 percent say "to unite us together in the Church"; 6 percent say "to heal the world"; 3 percent say "to guide the pope and the bishops" and 1 percent say "to heal sin."

But while Core Catholics have pluralistic views about God's relations with the world and humankind, there is virtual consensus on the image and characteristics of God, who is seen as all powerful and loving, not vindictive. Core Catholics overwhelmingly view God literally as a "father figure," choosing positive—and male—imagery to describe God (Table 22).

Table 22. **Core Catholic Descriptions of God**

DESCRIPTION	RESPONDENTS CALLING THIS DESCRIPTION "COMPLETELY ACCURATE" (%)
Creator	85
Father	76
Redeemer	76
Friend	74
Protector	68
Master	61
Lover	53
Judge	47
Mother	22

Similarly, when asked to describe God's attributes, Core Catholics first chose "Forgiving" (87 percent said this was "extremely true" for them). At the bottom of the list, only 5 to 6 percent said it was "extremely true" that God was indifferent, distant, or vindictive (Table 23).

Table 23. **Core Catholic Opinion on the Attributes of God**

ATTRIBUTE/DESCRIPTION	RESPONDENTS CALLING THIS ATTRIBUTE "EXTREMELY TRUE" FOR THEM (%)
Forgiving	87
Faithful	83
All powerful	82
Dependable	78
Aware of everything I think	75
Mysterious	65
Close	63

Attribute/Description	Respondents Calling This Attribute "Extremely True" for Them (%)
My constant companion	59
Awesome	57
A creative force in history	57
Fascinating	56
Clearly knowable	51
Judgmental	34
Strict	23
In my life more as a symbol or an ideal than as a real presence I can feel	13
Permissive	12
More present in relationships with others than in an individual's life	11
Distant	6
Vindictive	6
Indifferent	5

Given their descriptions of God, it is not surprising that Core Catholics feel close to God. There are some surprises, however, in the activities which make Core Catholics feel close to God. The study asked them to rate these activities on a scale 1 to 5, with 1 being "Not Close At All" and 5 being "Extremely Close." Table 24 gives a list of activities and the combined scores of 4 and 5.

Table 24. Core Catholic Experience of the Closeness of God, by Activity

Activity	Respondents Feeling Close to God During This Activity (%)*
Receiving Holy Communion	91
Praying privately	89
Being absolved or anointed, etc.	77
Helping individuals in need	71
Being with a person I love	68
Gathering with the congregation during Mass	65
Chanting and praying the liturgy	61
Working for justice and peace	52
Reading the gospels	48
Obeying church rules	42
Praying in a charismatic group	33

*These respondents rated this activity 4 or 5 on a scale of 1 to 5 in which 5 was the highest rating ("extremely close").

It is consistent that receiving Communion and praying privately make Core Catholics feel closer to God. Absolving and annointing are sacramental rituals, so it is expected that these also rank high. It is also no surprise that aspects relating to the Mass make Core Catholics feel closer to God. But the high ranking for "helping those in need," "being with a person I love," and "working for justice and peace" is definitely surprising; it indicates that Catholics continue to find God in communal, social activities and suggests that the church has only begun to tap the potential for involving Core Catholics in social action and promoting peace and justice.

While praying in a charismatic group ranks at the bottom of the list, the fact that 33 percent of Core Catholics say such an experience has made them feel close to God is quite significant. National Gallup surverys have found that no more than 4 percent of all Catholics consider themselves Charismatics. Yet one-third of Core Catholics praise such services, and even higher percentages have apparently participated in them. We saw earlier that 23 percent of United States parishes have Charismatic Renewal groups. All of this suggests that the charismatic movement has been politically adept in obtaining official recognition for a small minority. It also suggests that the movement has become a fixed element on the devotional and liturgical "smorgasboard" from which post-Vatican II Catholics nourish themselves spiritually.

One form of feeling closeness to God is a "religious experience." The study asked Core Catholics, "How often in your life have you had an experience where you felt as though you were very close to a powerful, spiritual force that seemed to lift you out of yourself?"

Fourty-four percent of Core Catholics said they had never had such an experience, but 27 percent said they had such an experience once or twice. Another 22 percent said they had had it several times, and 8 percent said they had had such experiences often.

Those saying they had had religious experiences cited a variety of triggering events. Key times in life were particularly significant—11 percent said they had a religious experience when they had been near death, 5 percent cited childbirth, and another 8 percent cited the more general category of "life passages." Nine percent said the trigger for a religious experience was private prayer outside of church, while 7 percent cited a church service.

CONCLUSIONS

Before the Vatican Council, the devotional life of American Catholics emphasized prayer to Mary and to various saints. It was replete with Benedictions, Novenas, Stations of the Cross, and other devotions. Catholics abstained from meat once a week and sometimes more. Confession was common.

A much different picture can be found among post-Vatican II Catholics, particularly younger Catholics. Prayer is much more likely to be directed to Jesus, the pre-Vatican II devotions are disappearing, and Confession and fasting are used only on special occasions. Much has been written about the supposed "protestantization" of American Catholicism. But it seems to be taking on some aspects of Judaism as well—the addition of a cantor and an emphasis on "High Holy Days" which eclipse weekly observances and mark the occasion of fasting and atonement.

The spiritual focus for the post-Vatican II Catholic is found in Sunday Mass, in receiving Communion, and in private prayer. There is very little in the way of small group devotion except among Charismatics. But it would be a serious mistake to dismiss the importance of private prayer to Core Catholics. When they rank private prayer high as a means of feeling close to God or of feeling fulfilled religiously, they are not providing lip service answers—they are describing an activity that they take very seriously and personally.

Post-Vatican II Catholic spirituality has a certain streamlined quality about it. It could well be argued that there is "less" devotional life today than before the Council. But it is by no means clear that "less" is really "less"—it may simply be different.

NOTE

This chapter is based on Report 6 by Mark Searle and David Leege. The report authors acknowledge comments and criticisms from Sister Kathleen Hughes of the Catholic Theological Union, University of Chicago; Father Robert Schmitz of the Cincinnati Archdiocesan Office of Planning and Research; and Sister Eleanor Bernstein of the Center for Pastoral Liturgy, University of Notre Dame. Additional material comes from the parishioner survey.

9. Education: Children, Teens, and Adults

The concept of education within Catholic parishes has undergone a major revolution in the United States, a revolution spurred by the Second Vatican Council. A century ago, Catholic education meant nuns teaching children the rudiments of the four Rs—readin', 'riting, 'rithmetic, and religion—in a parish school which served as a refuge from a hostile Protestant culture. Today, Catholic education at the parish level means religious education programs for grade schoolers, high schoolers, and adults. It may or may not mean a parish school, and, if it does, the majority of teachers are lay men and women and many of the students are non-Catholics. All of this takes place within a culture in which Catholics are full members.

Reams of pages have been written about the status and future of Catholic elementary and secondary education in the United States, and the Notre Dame study did not attempt to duplicate this volume of material. But the approach that the study took to parochial schools was unique—it focused on the role the parish school plays within parish life and within the context of parish education. This offers, as we shall see, some important new insights into both parish life and the Catholic educational system.

Before looking at the Notre Dame study findings on education and the parish, it is necessary to establish some perspective on the status of Catholic schools and education today. In the historical chapter, we have already seen the growth of the parochial school system in response to a hostile public school environment, the birth of the CCD program for religious education for Catholics in public school in the 1920s, the decline in Catholic school enrollment since the 1960s, and the shift from religious to lay teachers.

We can gain some additional insight from an overview contained in *United States Catholic Elementary and Secondary Schools 1985-1986,* published by the National Catholic Educational Association. According to the NCEA report, in the 1985–86 school year, there were 7,811 United States Catholic elementary schools with 2,061,000 students and 1,434 Catholic secondary schools with 760,000 students for a total of 9,245 schools with 2,821,000 students. These figures represent a decline of 348 elementary schools, 130 secondary schools, and 397,000 students since 1979. The Catholic school population declined by more than 2,000,000 between 1965 and 1978.

The declining enrollment in Catholic schools has come at a time of increasing enrollment in other church-related schools, particularly Baptist and fundamentalist institutions. In the 1965–66 school year, Catholic schools made up 87 percent of all private schools; by 1980–81 that had fallen to 63 percent. The percentage of students in private schools rose from 10.5 percent in 1970–71 to 12.6 percent in 1983. NCEA figures show that the Catholic school is a primarily a parish institution at the elementary school level, but not at the high school level (Table 25).

Table 25. **Sponsorship of Catholic Schools**

| | ELEMENTARY | | SECONDARY | |
| | 1970–71 | 1985–86 | 1970–71 | 1985–86 |
SPONSOR	(PERCENTAGE OF SCHOOLS)		(PERCENTAGE OF SCHOOLS)	
Single parish	92.6	87.0	23.2	14.9
Interparish	3.5	6.6	11.6	11.4
Diocesan	0.3	2.3	26.3	35.0
Private	3.6	4.1	38.9	38.7

Source: National Catholic Educational Association

Two related dramatic shifts in parochial schools involve higher percentages of both non-Catholic and minority students since the early 1970s. In the 1969–70 school year, only 2.7 percent of Catholic school students were non-Catholic; that figure rose to 11.1 percent in 1983–84, according to the NCEA. (The Notre Dame survey found 12 percent of parochial students were non-Catholic, statistically the same finding.) The percentage of Asian-American students in Catholic schools quintupled between 1970 and 1985, most likely reflecting the presence of Catholic refugees from Southeast Asia. Table 26 illustrates the sharp increase in minority enrollment.

Table 26. **Minority Enrollment in Catholic Schools**

	1970–71	1984–85
	ELEMENTARY	
	(PERCENTAGE OF TOTAL ENROLLMENT)	
Black	5.12	9.11
Hispanic	5.30	9.71
	SECONDARY	
Black	3.72	7.32
Hispanic	3.82	7.45
	ALL SCHOOLS	
Black	4.80	8.62
Hispanic	4.96	9.13

Neither the NCEA nor the United States Catholic Conference has comparable national figures to profile religious education in the United States. Here the Notre Dame study information is unique; it reveals the widespread presence of religious education programs in American parishes. Religious education for grade school children is a staple of the Catholic parishes studied—93 percent have such programs, including even the smallest parishes which offer virtually no other programs or services than Sunday Mass and religious education. There is a slight falloff in religious education programs for high school students—84 percent of parishes report such programs.

One surprise is that 63 percent of United States parishes report having programs of adult religious education. This is clearly a growth area in the American Catholic church. Adult religious education received an impetus from Vatican II. Follow-up to the United States bishops 1983 pastoral letter, *The Challenge of Peace,* and their 1986 pastoral letter on the United States economy, is likely to feed this growth.

Given the greater resources required to run a parish grade school than to run a religious education program, it is not surprising that fewer parishes have their own grade schools. But overall, almost half of all parishes—45 percent—do have their own schools. David Leege's analysis of the relationship between parish complexity and parish programs showed that schools are much more likely to be found in the larger, more complex parishes.

The Notre Dame study reveals that education is the focus of a considerable amount of parish activity—14 percent of Core Catholics in the sample are involved in education. This ranks behind only the 22 percent involved in social or recreational activities and the 19 percent involved in liturgy. Both parish schools and CCD programs serve to involve parish members in the life of the church.

This involvement is reflected in the fact that education programs rank behind only bingo as the best-attended activities in the parish: 21 percent of pastors and parish administrators in the 1,099 parish survey list adult religious education as one of the best-attended programs; 20 percent cite religious education for children, and 17 percent cite parish school activities and sports. The fact that half as many parishes have grade schools as have CCD programs, yet school activity is cited about as often as religious education as a parish draw, indicates that schools may stimulate proportionately more lay involvement. At the same time, the presence of adult religious education programs balances off this greater involvement.

A similar pattern is found in pastor and parish administrator responses concerning the activities which serve as a source of parish vitality. Education programs rank at the top: 25 percent cite children's religious education programs, 24 percent cite parish school activities and sports, and 20 percent cite adult religious education.

Despite the role schools and religious education play in spurring parish vitality, parish schools do not serve as a magnet attracting new members. Only 2 percent of Core Catholics said they attend the parish church they attend in order to get their children admitted to the parish school.

THE PARISH GRADE SCHOOL

The Notre Dame study offers important information about the shape of parish grade schools and their staffing. In the survey of 1,099 parishes, the average school has 293 students, down from 305 students five years ago (which would be 1978). About four students in five (78 percent) live within the parish borders. Twelve percent of students are not Catholic. Five percent of United States parishes have only one paid staff member at their school; 7 percent have two paid staff members; 8 percent have three; 7 percent have four; and 13 percent have five or more paid staffers. Only 6 percent of parishioners say they speak frequently with the principal of the parish school, and 10 percent say they speak frequently with teachers at the school.

Those responding to the parishioner's questionnaire were asked to agree or disagree with a number of statements describing their parish school. Those statements and responses, with percentages adjusted to total 100 percent to reflect responses from only those who have parish schools, are shown in Table 27.

Table 27. **Core Catholic Opinion of Parish Schools**

STATEMENT	YES (%)	NO (%)
The parish school offers better academic training than other schools	67	33
The parish school has higher quality teachers than other schools	49	51
The parish school offers daily instruction in religion	92	8
The parish school provides a more disciplined environment than other schools	85	15

STATEMENT	YES (%)	NO (%)
The parish school displays more concern for the students than is true in other schools	75	25
The parish school teaches values I want instilled in my children	92	8
The parish school has better students than other schools	43	57

These responses reveal several important patterns. First, it is clear that, to Core Catholics, the major distinguishing characteristic of their parish grade school is the presence of daily religious instruction and the teaching of values they view as important—more than 90 percent of Core Catholics with parish schools report these qualities. This should not be surprising, given the fact that these are the elements which church and church school officials believe represent that most basic difference between parochial and other schools. Nevertheless, these findings should be reassuring because they indicate that Catholic parishioners do, in fact, find these qualities in their parish schools.

The next most commonly cited characteristic of parish schools is "a more disciplined environment than other schools." This reflects and confirms the conventional wisdom that parochial schools are stricter and more demanding than other schools. The 85 percent citing discipline in their parish schools is close to the 75 percent who report a greater concern for students in their parish schools than in other schools. This again confirms the conventional wisdom—in this case, the belief that Catholic schools have a more personal dimension that do other schools.

The 67 percent of Core Catholics with parish schools who say their schools offer better academic training than other schools reflects confidence in the school's mission—and in their sense of discipline and personal concern for students. But Core Catholics are evenly divided on the question of whether the teachers in their schools are of higher quality than those in other schools. This may indicate simply a vote of confidence in public school teachers, or it may reflect a sense that parochial school teachers are not outstanding. This finding suggests that to Core Catholics, it is the school vision and atmosphere, not the quality of its teachers, which makes them distinctive. This conclusion is supported by the fact that 57 percent of Core Catholics with parish schools disagree with the statement that the students in their schools are better than those in other schools. This finding reflects a realistic assessment of all students—as well as the fact that many Core Catholics have one child in a parochial school and another in a public school.

These patterns are reflected again when parishioners with children in parish schools were asked to pick the most important reason for sending their children there. The most common reasons cited were religious instruction and the teaching of values; least often cited were academic quality, discipline, and concern about students.

Those parishioners with school-age children who did not send their children to the parish school cited two main reasons about equally—finances and a "bad attitude" at the school. The references to a "bad attitude" reflect the tensions sometimes found between parish and school, pastor, and principal. The percent citing finances as a reason for not sending their children to the parish school—4 percent of all parishioners—is fairly small and raises questions about whether new forms of financial aid would significantly affect the number of students attending parish grade schools.

PARISH RELIGIOUS EDUCATION

The average parish surveyed has 202 grade school students and 67 high school students in religious education programs. There are also an average of 87 adults in religious education programs. Half of the adult religious education programs combine a variety of approaches. In addition, 17 percent involve instruction on specific topics, 15 percent involve Bible study, 7 percent involve sacramental preparation for adults, 3 percent involve sacramental preparation for children, and 3 percent involve spiritual development.

Twenty-two percent of parishes have one paid staff member in religious education, 5 percent have two staff members, 2 percent have three, 1 percent has four, and 2 percent have five or more.

Core Catholics give religious education a high priority in their parishes. As noted earlier, when Core Catholics were asked to rank ten items on a scale of 1 to 5 (with 3 indicating the parish should give the item the same priority it is giving it now, 1 indicating the lowest priority, and 5 the highest) religious education and help for poor people within the parish ranked at the top. Religious education for teenagers, with an average score of 4.04, was the top priority, followed by religious education for preteens (3.88), helping the poor within the parish (3.82), making converts and/or reclaiming dropouts (3.70), and religious education for adults (3.64). One Core Catholic in four views religious education as a primary purpose of the parish itself.

CASE STUDIES

Some of the most interesting information about parish education contained in the Notre Dame study comes from comments made by on-site observers at the thirty-six parishes selected for in-depth study. Here are some anecdotes, case studies, from these reports:

• A northeastern suburban church offers an example of a successful school in a successful parish. The school was praised by townspeople who were not members of the parish. The school had three-hundred students in kindergarten through eighth grade. The principal said that children in all grades consistently test six months to one year above their actual grades. This difference occurred despite the fact that the student-teacher ratio at the school—30:1—was higher than desired levels.

"Another set of variables may well account for the success of the school, as well as the remarkable test scores," the observer suggested. "These elements could be grouped under the rubric of 'social cohesion.' First, there is a great deal of parental support for the school that goes far beyond the normal perfunctory attendance at PTA meetings, etc. The faculty, and especially the principal, have taken pains to meet with every parent of every child to explain to them what is expected of them and their child as well as the philosophy of the school. Second, the faculty is a very tight-knit and dedicated group who as a whole are concerned for the school and for the students. (It is significant to note that faculty salaries at $8,000 to $11,000 annually are greatly below the level of the public schools, but the teachers do not mind this greatly as there has been a very low turnover rate. I believe they consider their job as a mission).

"Another factor leading to social cohesion is of course the religious emphasis which consists of formal religious instruction as well as a good deal of everyday religious emphasis such as prayer for a sick child. Also, the priests (three) teach classes at the school and are usually involved with the school's welfare."

• In a northwestern suburban parish, the school was well run and was administered separately, for the most part, from parish administration and finances. Almost half of the student body—forty-five percent—was non-Catholic and the school was in many ways a model of integration. The parish laity was quite active in the school: parish bingo subsidized most of the operating costs. The lay faculty was extremely committed. The school had a peace program designed by a local teacher. Only thirty children from the parish attended public school, and there was no separate religious education program for them.

• In another northwestern suburban parish, the school was also a great source of pride. Parishioners and teachers proudly reported that the enrollment and the quality of education had steadily improved since the arrival of a new pastor six years earlier. About half the children in grades one through eight in the parish attended the school, and only eleven families who were not members of the parish had children in the school. The school was run almost entirely by the local parish. Only one teacher was non-Catholic, and most of the teachers were members of the parish. A staff of parish volunteers helped with lunch duty, playground duty, library duty, remedial reading, fund raising, office work, and sports—there were thirty volunteer coaches for twelve sports teams. An active home-school association kept parents involved. One year, the staff identified a need to communicate more clearly with parents about the nature and content of religious instruction. They made this the subject of fall in-service training. A parishioner recently embellished the school hallways with graphics.

• The school also had a strong religious education program and a special Mass was held for the school children on Fridays—the students themselves planned the Mass twice a month. The school had provided a strong education program for the children, it had activated parishioners and integrated them into the parish and it had helped to set goals for the parish.

• The school was a definite rallying point of parish life. When more than two-hundred CCD students were added to the equation, it was clear that the parish's newborn catechetical thrust was reaching a significant part of the parish population. In fact, most parish leaders identified catechetical ministry as the obvious center of the parish's mission.

• In a south Atlantic suburban parish, the only paid staff member was the religious education coordinator. The haphazard participation in other church activities contrasted sharply to the way CCD was run. All volunteer teachers were required to take the Teachers' Learning Program and were later periodically screened "to see if they are following the book." The value of such structured training for the children has been impressed upon the parents, resulting in a high rate of registration and attendance for CCD in all grades through high school. The benefits provided by the CCD program were more pervasive than simply providing solid religious education for the children; the adults of the parish bonded together as they shared the same physical space for some time every Sunday while their children received instruction. There were no Masses scheduled during the CCD sessions to insure that the young people would have an opportunity each week to attend Mass.

• In a midwestern suburban parish, the school, apart from a period in the late sixties through early seventies when it experienced major upheavals and the loss of parishioners' confidence, had been a continuing parish priority. It continued as the center of parish activity at the time of the study, arguably operating as the principal "draw" for families of school-age children.

The notion that this school stood at the center of parish life gains credence from a number of indicators. Liturgy was not a draw; the liturgies were quite bad, and the church was almost empty by the official end of the Mass. Religious education programs tailored to adults had largely flopped. The school reflected the socio-economic isolation of this upper-middle-class parish. Virtually no non-Catholic students attended the school, apparently because of a tuition schedule which strongly favored parish members.

• In a rural midwestern parish, the school was in a process of revitalization following a decline in the midseventies and early eighties. The decline was caused by the departure of religious teachers; parishioners' inability to pay tuition; the presence of a strong, modern public school system; and an indecisive principal. At the time of the study, a new principal was working to restore the school.

ATTITUDES TOWARD EDUCATION ISSUES

Core Catholics hold basically conservative attitudes on a number of social issues related to education, as is shown in Table 28.

Table 28. **Attitude of Core Catholics on Social Issues Related to Education**

STATEMENT	STRONGLY AGREE (%)	AGREE (%)	DISAGREE (%)	STRONGLY DISAGREE (%)
Parents should have the right to censor textbooks and books selected for the public library	15	45	29	11

Statement	Strongly Agree (%)	Agree (%)	Disagree (%)	Strongly Disagree (%)
Schools share with parents the responsibility for educating children in sexuality	17	63	16	4
Secular humanism has greatly eroded the moral fiber of our society	18	50	28	3
The government should let parents deduct some of the costs of sending their children to parochial schools	38	45	12	5
Prayer should be required in Public schools	23	47	26	5
Public schools should be required to give equal time for the teaching of creation theory and evolution theory about man's origins	16	51	26	7
Homosexuals should be allowed to teach in public schools	3	32	40	25
Busing should be used to achieve racial integration in the public schools	4	22	44	30

Some of the findings are not surprising, for example, the strong support for tax aid for parents of students in parochial schools. The strong opposition to busing and the presence of homosexual teachers in the public schools also offer no surprise.

One possible surprise is the strong support for sex education in the schools—as long as parents are involved. It may well be that parental involvement rather than censorship is what Core Catholics have in mind when they agree that parents should be able to "censor" textbooks and library books. Similarly, concern about "secular humanism" reflects a general sense that traditional values are threatened in American society more than a support for a fundamentalist attack on a so-called secular humanism conspiracy against religious beliefs.

The support for equal time for "creation theory" is another surprise, particular because Catholics generally have no problem in reconciling the physical process of evolution with their faith. The response probably reflects lack of awareness of the political debate over the teaching of "creation science" in the public schools, a sensitivity to religious concerns, and the general Catholic preference for pluralism.

Finally, the support for school prayer is not surprising because it reflects the findings of national opinion surveys over a number of years. It is noteworthy for its irony, however, given the fact that it was the dominance of distinctly Protestant prayers in the public schools which led to the creation of the parochial school system in the first place.

Education ranks high as a priority for the parish in its dealings with the broader community. Asked to indicate which of eight community activities they would like to see their parish emphasize more, only prevention of drug and alcohol abuse ranked ahead of efforts to improve the quality of public education. Almost half of Core Catholics—46 percent—said they wanted to see their parish give quality public education a higher priority, 35 percent were satisfied with what the parish was doing, and only 19 percent wanted public education to be a lower priority.

CONCLUSIONS

Information surfaced by the Notre Dame study makes it abundantly clear that for Core Catholics, education is a high priority. But there are two important new dimensions to this priority. First, education is now seen as a "womb-to-tomb" concern, a priority for adults growing in their faith as well as for young children being introduced to it. Second, Core Catholics see two dimensions to education—religious education and basic education. And they are perfectly happy to have their children obtain it in one of two ways—in a high quality parish school or through a combination of high quality public schools and parish CCD programs.

The historical part of the study also sheds important light on the role of Catholic schools today. The major impetus to the beginning of the Catholic school system was the existence of a public school system in which Protestantism was the de facto religion and Catholics were second-class citizens. That is no longer the case, and there is no need for parochial schools to serve as the refuge they once were. In fact, the declining share of private school enrollment in Catholic schools and the increasing share of fundamentalist schools reflects the fact that Catholics are now in the mainstream of society and Fundamentalists are outside of it.

The increase in enrollment in Catholic schools by minorities and non-Catholics reflects other significant shifts in Catholic parish life. The increase in Hispanic enrollment simply reflects service to the growing Hispanic Catholic community. But the high percentage of non-Catholic black students reflects the growing service parochial schools perform for inner-city blacks, the first time Catholic schools have existed largely to serve a non-Catholic population.

The increased lay staffing of parochial schools offers a significant avenue to lay leadership in the church—as well as increased opportunity for conflict with pastors.

But we have seen that both parish schools and religious education programs serve as sources of parish vitality and means of stimulating greater parish involvement. These are positive roles. Yet both programs, particularly schools, can also serve as the focus of parish discontent. The nature of the parish calls for some form of religious education program, while parish schools are much more of an option. We can conclude that the parish school is neither necessary nor sufficient to insure parish vitality. Many parishes are successful due to the existence of their schools, but there are also thriving, vital parishes without schools and dying, dry parishes with schools.

Until now, the Catholic school system has been approached as if it were a system in the same sense as, say, the New York City public school system. But, in fact, at the grade school level it is really a collection of schools which are part of individual parishes and are shaped by their individual histories, circumstances, and changing fortunes. Anyone who wants to study the state and future of the Catholic school system must first understand parish life.

All of the information from the Notre Dame study indicates that education—religious and secular, in parochial and public schools—is a high priority for American Catholics active in parish life. It also indicates a continuing place for the parish school. But schools will be opened or closed depending on the conditions in each individual parish. Core Catholics value parochial grade schools—as an option.

NOTE

Material in this chapter is based on the parishioner survey and on-site reports.

10. The Parish: Ecumenism, Evangelization, and Social Action

We have often referred to the parish as a community. But while the parish does function as a community, it also exists within a wider community—in a specific city, in a specific state, in a specific country. We have emphasized that parish life is shaped by the personalities of individual leaders, but it is also shaped by geography, economics, ethnicity, population density, and the proportion of Catholics in the general population.

The parish is also part of its community, relating to it and serving it in a variety of ways. It becomes involved in community problems, and its members care deeply about local, national, and international issues. Catholic parishes never operated in isolation from their surrounding community, even in the days when they served as a refuge from a society ill disposed towards immigrants. In that period, the parish served to socialize immigrant Catholics into their new home.

But Vatican II gave a strong impetus to the entire church, and therefore the parish, to become even more deeply engaged in the world. In particular, the Council opened up a new horizon by reaching out to those of other faiths and no faith, and particularly by embracing ecumenism, openness toward and cooperation with other Christian churches with the goal of eventual reunion. Another spur to greater involvement was a commitment to greater involvement in the battle for human rights in the secular world, including an emphasis on structural change and human development.

ECUMENISM

Ecumenism has been one of the more popular of the Vatican II reforms. On the international and national levels, it has meant official "dialogues" between Catholics and a variety of Protestant denominations discussing areas of agreement and disagreement in theology. It has also stimulated close relations with the Jewish people. At the national, state, and metropolitan levels, ecumenism has meant increased cooperation on matters of community concern—from national economic and foreign policy issues to neighborhood concerns. Some seventy-one Catholic dioceses in thirty states are full members of local councils of churches. At the parish level, the ecumenical movement has meant increased contact with neighboring churches for worship, community service, and socializing.

The Notre Dame study found widespread acceptance of ecumenism among Core Catholics and a considerable amount of ecumenical activity at the parish level. For example, the parishioner survey found strong support among Core Catholics for intercommunion with non-Catholic Christians: 70 percent of Core Catholics supported intercommunion, despite official church policy restricting intercommunion to members of those non-Catholic churches who share the Catholic church's belief in the meaning of the Eucharist.

The survey also found that Core Catholics viewed improving contacts with non-Catholic churches within their neighborhoods as a parish priority: 38 percent said they wanted their parish to make this a higher priority, 48 percent said they were satisfied with what their parish was doing, and only 15 percent said they wanted a lower priority for ecumenism.

The Core Catholics surveyed are quite comfortable discussing religion with non-Catholics. We noted earlier that while Core Catholics are most likely to discuss their religious beliefs with other Cathlics with similar beliefs, they are as likely to discuss their faith with non-Catholics holding similar religious views as they are to discuss it with Catholics with differing views.

Some of the most useful information about ecumenism at the parish level came from the on-site observers who visited the 36-parish sample. These reports indicate the importance of neighborhood life and history in supporting ecumenical activity:

- In a midwestern suburban parish in a community heavily influenced by evangelical Christians, the previous pastor tried to keep his congregation insulated. After he died, his successor tried a different approach, reaching out to other Christian churches. He joined the local ministerial alliance and established closer ties with local Methodist and Episcopal churches. The congregation has taken part in joint activities with other churches, running a food pantry and supporting the Nuclear Freeze movement and local fair housing programs.
- In a small, rural community in the intermountain region, the Catholic parish operated within a heavily Protestant setting; half of the entire community was Methodist. But there was a great deal of cooperation with the local Methodist church: ecumenical services on Thanksgiving and ecumenical choir meetings on an irregular basis. Whenever possible, the Methodist pastor and Catholic priest planned their liturgies together. Occasionally, the Methodist pastor brought his entire congregation to Sunday Mass. The Methodist pastor was very supportive of the United States bishops' peace pastoral, but the high degree of ecumenical cooperation was not due to the attitudes of the pastors alone— it reflected a strong lay commitment. Members of both congregations remembered a time more than a decade before when the Methodist church had an anti-Catholic pastor who placed loudspeakers on his church so that he could direct his anti-Catholic sermons to the whole community. His congregation rebelled and refused to go to church until he was replaced. At the time of our study, lay people ran an ecumenical youth ministry and Bible study without any guidance from either pastor.
- In another intermountain parish, in a small town, the laypeople who had dominated church affairs for decades were also re-

sponsible for an ecumenical agenda which featured cooperation with virtually every denomination except Jehovah's Witnesses. The parish had held joint programs with mainline Protestant churches, Baptists, Mormons, and Seventh-day Adventists. There were close ties with an Episcopal church whose members attended the Catholic parish's lay ministry training program. When the Catholic and Lutheran pastors were unsure about whether a joint Advent choir was a good idea, the laity in both churches insisted that it was and made the idea a reality.

• In a rural northwestern parish, the cooperation with the only other Christian church in the area—a United Church of Christ which combined former UCC, Baptist, and Methodist congregations—was remarkable. The two parishes ran a joint emergency bank account for the community. When one pastor visited the hospital, he visited the parishioners of the other. Similarly, when one pastor greeted newcomers who preferred the "opposing" church, he provided them the other pastor's phone number and a schedule of church services. There was a joint Thanksgiving service and a joint Palm Sunday service. The Palm Sunday service began with a blessing of the palms by both pastors in the Catholic parish hall, included a procession down the town's main street to the UCC church for prayers and reflections, and was followed by a reception in the church basement. Each pastor distributed Communion to members of his congregation, who marched down the aisle in two lines. When there was confusion between the lines, the pastors used the occasion to make the point that it is indeed clumsy and uncomfortable to be separated.

The material on ecumenism gathered by the Notre Dame study provides another reminder of the impact of history, environment, and personality on parish life. There is broad support for increased ecumenical activity on the part of Core Catholics, who want to go beyond the official church in their outreach to other denominations. But ecumenical activity becomes a reality within the concrete life of each parish when a pastor talks with ministers from other denominations, when parish leaders reach out, and when people in the same community know one another.

EVANGELIZATION

Catholic "evangelization" seems at first a contradiction in terms. Catholics have never practiced and have themselves been repulsed by the sometimes heavy-handed proselytizing of evangelical and fundamentalist Christians. But since the late 1970s, Catholics have themselves talked about evangelization which complements the ecumenical movement—it reaches out to lapsed and fallen-away Catholics and extends an invitation to unchurched Americans.

On the surface, evangelization appears popular with Core Catholics: 86 percent believe the church should place more emphasis on spreading the faith, and 53 percent believe reaching out to dropouts and making converts should be a higher priority for their parish. But only 2 percent of Core Catholics are personally involved in evangelization, and only 32 percent of Catholic parishes have formal evangelization programs, the same percentage having formal programs for the Rite of Christian Initiation for Adults (RCIA).

Evangelization and RCIA programs are found most often in minority parishes: 66 percent of black parishes and 47 percent of Hispanic parishes have both programs. Among other ethnic groups, 36 percent of Irish parishes have evangelization programs, and 34 percent have RCIA programs, while other groups are less likely to have these programs. Evangelization and RCIA programs are heavily concentrated in the south Atlantic region, with half of the parishes in those regions having them. In general, RCIA is found most often in places with low Catholic populations.

We noted earlier that David Leege found four basic types of parish, ranging from the simplest, which provide little more than Sunday Mass and religious education for children, to the more complex, which offer a broad array of programs and services. Only the most complex parishes have evangelization and RCIA programs. It is difficult to conclude too much from these findings. But it seems safe to say that while Core Catholics support evangelization in theory, it appears in practice primarily in those parishes which serve blacks and Hispanics, in non-Catholic areas, and in parishes which already have a large number of other programs.

SOCIAL SERVICE, SOCIAL ACTION, AND THE PARISH

Social service and social action are two related but different elements of involvement with the broader community within the life of American Catholic parishes. Social service refers to the kinds of activity generally known as charity—feeding the hungry, sheltering the homeless, collecting clothing for the needy, running health clinics. The element of social service goes back at least a century in American Catholic parishes. We have seen how the Saint Vincent de Paul Society and other parish-based organizations emerged in the mid-nineteenth century to meet the needs of poor immigrants, victims of the Depression, and minorities.

Social action is a bit newer. It involves efforts to change social structures and institutions to make them more just. Catholics have long been involved in such efforts through the political system, the labor movement, the civil rights and anti-Vietnam War movements, and through neighborhood organizations. But it was the Second Vatican Council's emphasis on engaging the world and seeking justice and peace that made social action a parish priority. Consequently, any evaluation of the place of social action programs in the parish must take into consideration this relatively short time frame.

Certainly the charitable side of parish life is a high priority for Core Catholics and their parishes. We have already seen, for example, that 33 percent of Core Catholics cite charitable works and help for those in need as the top priority for the parish. This ranks behind only the 42 percent who cited the parish as the People of God or some other aspect of community and is statistically tied with the 32 percent who make general references to the parish as the center of religious activity. As a parish priority, charity ranks higher than focus on the sacraments and liturgy, personal spiritual growth, and the preservation and propagation of the Roman Catholic faith.

We have also already seen that 52 percent of the United States parishes in our sample have social service programs. These programs rank ninth, in frequency, behind religious education for grade school and high school, a parish council, a liturgy planning group, a program for the sick, adult religious education, youth ministry, and ministry to the aged. It ranks ahead of music and cultural activities, marriage and family development, prayer and small reflection groups, parish grade schools, ministry training programs, a parish planning process, the catechumenate, evangelization, parish renewal, parish leadership training, charismatic renewal, ministry to the separated and divorced, and social action. Twenty percent of American Catholic parishes have a social action program. This is tied with programs for the separated and divorced as the least common parish program.

Organized social service programs are most likely to be found along the middle and Southeastern seaboard (77 percent), in the suburbs (65 percent), cities (60 percent), and in black (79 percent) and Irish (62 percent) parishes. They are least likely to be found in the mountain (47 percent) and Midwestern (44 percent) parishes.

Social action programs follow a similar pattern, but trailed by 20 to 40 percentage points. They are most likely to be found in black (55 percent), Hispanic (27 percent), and Irish (23 percent) parishes. There is a sharp division along geographic lines: 29 percent of urban and 27 percent of suburban parishes have social action programs, while in small towns and rural areas, the figure drops to 11 percent.

Twenty percent seems low on the face of it. But we must ask, what proportion of parishes would have had such a program before Vatican II? We can only guess, but it is likely that only a handful of parishes would have had justice and peace programs a generation ago. There are several other encouraging signs. For example, while it is not surprising that Leege found that black parishes were more likely to have social action programs, it is surprising that he found that 27 percent of suburban parishes had social action programs. This indicates that those programs are growing in the area of the church that is growing the fastest.

Leege also found social action programs in the most complex parishes. This suggests that it is not lack of interest that prevents a parish from having a social action program, but lack of resources. Social action is seen as a proper activity for the church and the parish, but one which is demanding and comes after more traditional programs such as religious education; ministry to the sick, young, and aged; liturgical planning; and social services.

The level of attention paid to social action within the parish may be related to the beliefs Core Catholics hold about the best way to approach social problems. The Notre Dame study asked Core Catholics to pick between two alternative statements: 62 percent agreed that "social problems can be solved best by first focusing on changing the hearts (that is, attitudes, beliefs, consciences) of individuals"; 38 percent agreed that "social problems can be solved best by first focusing on transforming human institutions and environments in which people live." There is no "correct" answer. When the World Synod of Bishops addressed the issue in the 1983 Synod on Reconciliation, their own answer was that both priorities must be emphasized simultaneously. It seems likely that if Core Catholics approach a 50-50 split on this question, action for social change will take on a higher priority within the parish.

Other findings from the Notre Dame study provide valuable insight into the attitudes of Core Catholics toward social service and social action and the role they play in the parish. First, helping poor people within the parish ranks behind only religious education as a parish priority: 60 percent of Core Catholics cited that as a high priority, and only 3 percent cited it as a low one. This contrasted sharply with helping the poor outside the parish: 32 percent saw this as a high priority, 15 percent as a low one. This might seem at first to suggest a callousness toward the poor who live outside the parish. But it is also likely that, because the question was asked within a parish context, Core Catholics gave a lower priority to helping the poor outside the parish simply because they assume that those poor are in someone else's parish, where they can more properly be served.

The same question found that 37 percent of Core Catholics favored placing a higher priority on "working to change unjust socioeconomic conditions," while 21 percent wanted a lower priority for such activity. Again, this is encouraging given the relatively short period of time in which a structural approach to justice issues has been a church priority.

An even more striking—in fact, stunning—finding comes in responses to a question about what activities make Core Catholics feel close to God. Receiving Communion, praying privately, and being absolved or annointed were the most often cited. But "helping individuals in need" ranked fourth, with 71 percent of Core Catholics saying this made them feel close to God. "Working for justice and peace" was cited by 52 percent of Core Catholics as an activity which made them feel close to God. This ranked ahead of reading the Gospels, obeying church rules, and praying in a charismatic group. The fact that half of Core Catholics feel closer to God while working for justice and peace indicates that the church's post-Vatican II emphasis on social justice is reaching into the consciousness of American Catholics.

It is still true, however, as we noted earlier, that there is a gap between rhetoric and reality when it comes to social service and social action within the parish. For example, despite the high percentages of Core Catholics citing social service and social action as a priority, only 4 percent of Core Catholics are involved in social action, welfare, or justice issues within the parish. This suggests several explanations. First, it could be that support for social service and social action has reached the lip service stage in which people feel pressured to speak positively about it, but not compelled to do anything about it. Another possible explanation is that parish structures have simply not yet caught up to parishioner interest. It is also possible that parish involvement does not reflect the fact that many Core Catholics are involved in social action pursuits outside of parish structures.

Social service and social action rank near the bottom of parish activities cited by pastors and parish administrators as a source of vitality for the parish. Nevertheless, 10 percent cite social service and 8 percent cite social action as a source of vitality, slightly more than the 7 percent who cited liturgical preparation as a source of parish vitality. In fact, given the fact that only 20 percent of parishes have social action programs, the 8 percent citing them as a source of parish vitality is impressive.

The Notre Dame study's on-site visits produced evidence that social service and social action contribute to parish vitality. One parish in the south Atlantic region stood out. The parish had historically been socially aware; it was marked by great dissension during the Vietnam War. A new staff member headed a Human Concerns Committee which encouraged people to go out into their communities and directly address issues of social injustice. One major project was resettlement of Vietnamese refugees. Another was a nonprofit corporation which was building housing for the elderly in cooperation with other parishes and the diocese. The pastor believed that, in addition to meeting a practical need, the housing would also be a source of education for the congregation and a way to provide a sense of home in a heavily mobile area. Parish leaders saw social action and involvement in local community problems as central to the parish's identity. They timed the construction of the housing for the elderly to coincide with the construction of a new worship area so that human and worship needs would not be seen in opposition.

What kind of community activities do Core Catholics want to become a higher priority for their parish? At the top of the list is (Table 29) an issue which also topped the list of issues on which we found a parish "opportunity gap," because large numbers of Core Catholics said they would turn to the parish for help if it were available—prevention of drug and alcohol abuse.

Table 29. **Core Catholic Opinion on Parish Involvement in Community Issues**

ISSUE	THINK PARISH SHOULD BE MORE INVOLVED (%)	THINK PARISH SHOULD BE LESS INVOLVED (%)
Prevention of drug/alcohol abuse	67	13
Quality of public education	47	19
Medical care	37	22
Rights of minorities	28	23
Handling of crime and criminals	28	30
Local elections	16	46
Business-government partnerships	14	46
Local zoning laws	13	49

We have already noted the priority Core Catholics give to quality public education. On only two other issues do Core Catholics seem to want more parish involvement—health care and support for the rights of minorities. Given the overrepresentation of blacks within the Core Catholic sample, the 28–23 percent margin supporting greater support for minority rights is probably somewhat greater than it would be among white, non-Hispanic Core Catholics alone.

This question surfaces some of the ambiguity about race which emerged among Core Catholics in the Notre Dame study. On one hand, large percentages of Core Catholics view racial discrimination as a sin—one as serious as abortion—and believe interracial marriages are morally acceptable. On the other hand, there is not a great deal of support for efforts specifically designed to help members of minority groups. This ambiguity is reflected in reports on on-site visits. One northwestern parish ran a school that was a model of integration, while one midwestern parish ran a school that was a virtual haven from integration. Some parishes had good relations with minority groups, while one northeastern parish regarded itself as virtually in a war zone surrounded by hostile Hispanics. Our study found a reservoir of good will on race relations within Core Catholics.

MIXING RELIGION AND POLITICS

In 1980, the United States bishops began work on two companion pastoral letters, one on peace (published in 1983) and one on the American economic system (published in 1986). These pastoral letters, coupled with the church's high visibility in the anti-abortion movement and in opposition to United States policy in Central America, have kept the church at the heart of the running debate on the "mixing" of religion and politics in America.

A question emerged from the discussion of these issues: With what degree of authority do the bishops speak when they address the moral dimension of political issues? In both pastorals, the bishops emphasized that the church speaks with greater authority on issues of general principle—such as its prohibition on the direct taking of innocent human life—than on more specific questions—such as support for an American-Soviet bilateral freeze on the production, testing, and deployment of nuclear weapons. But some questioned whether the bishops should address such issues at all. Some held that they should leave those subjects to the individual consciences of lay Catholics. When the bishops speak as a national conference on the obligations of citizens in an election year, they urge Catholics to study candidates character and positions on a wide range of issues and to vote their conscience.

The Notre Dame study asked Core Catholics which level of authority—the pope, the United States bishops, priests, or the individual Catholic—should address a variety of political issues (Table 30). Obviously, some felt that more than one level of authority should address the issues.

Table 30. Core Catholic Opinion on the Church Addressing
Political Issues

ISSUE	POPE SHOULD SPEAK (%)	BISHOPS SHOULD SPEAK (%)	PRIESTS SHOULD SPEAK (%)	INDIVIDUAL JUDGMENT (%)
Aid to poor countries	70	47	41	17
Eliminating poverty from this country	32	67	48	17
Birth control	41	22	26	54
Equal opportunity for advancement regardless of worker's sex	31	38	39	43
Sex and violence on TV	28	45	52	38
Action for world disarmament	74	38	33	24
Racial integration	42	46	45	34

Several patterns are apparent. Core Catholics seem to regard the
level of authority used in addressing social and political issues in
terms of the scope of the problem. For example, they are more
likely to want the pope to address the questions of disarmament
and world poverty—issues with clearly global dimensions. When
it comes to poverty in the United States, however, the preference
shifts to the United States bishops as the best voice to address
what is perceived as a national problem. Similarly, sex and violence on television seems to be perceived as a national, rather than
an international, issue.

There are only two issues on which Core Catholics are more
likely to want to rely on individual Catholics than on the pope,
bishops, or priests. One involves equal job opportunities for
women. Here the margin is slim, and about four Core Catholics
in ten believe bishops, priests, and individuals should address the
issue. Again, the lower percentage wanting the pope to speak on
the issue seems to reflect the perception that this is a national, not
an international, issue.

But the remaining issue which Core Catholics prefer to leave to the individual is an important one—birth control. More than half of Core Catholics (54 percent) want this issue to be left to individual Catholics, and only 22 percent want the bishops to speak out on it. The 43 percent who say the pope should speak on birth control reflects the fact that this is perceived as an issue for the whole church, not just American Catholics. But the percentage of Core Catholics who want the pope to speak out on birth control is still considerably less than the percentage who want him to speak out on world poverty and disarmament. Similarly, Core Catholics would much rather hear the United States bishops speak about poverty in this country than about birth control. These findings reinforce the earlier Notre Dame study finding that most Core Catholics reject the church's teaching on birth control. But they also give strong support to the notion that Core Catholics want their church to address major issues of peace and poverty.

Seven Core Catholics in ten (69 percent) agreed that "religious organizations should try to persuade senators, representatives, or city council members to enact legislation they would like to see become law"; 31 percent disagree. But this support must be seen in the context of two other findings. First, the study asked Core Catholics the degree to which their religious beliefs guide or influence their voting decisions. Nine percent said, "My voting decisions are completely determined by my religious beliefs and values"; 34 percent said they were influenced by their religious beliefs "to a large degree"; 35 percent said they were influenced "only to a small degree"; and 21 percent said their voting decisions were "not at all" influenced by their religious beliefs.

It is impossible to deduce from this just what Core Catholics mean when they say their voting is influenced by their religious beliefs. Are they influenced in a general way, or by a candidate's stand on specific issues of concern to the church? In any event, about forty percent of Core Catholics attach great importance to their religious views when they enter the voting booth.

The other relevant findings concern Core Catholic clear preference for less, rather than more, involvement in local elections:

46 percent wanted less involvement, and only 16 percent wanted more parish involvement in local elections. These questions taken together suggest that Core Catholics want their church to address major social and political issues and support the church's right to lobby on such issues of concern. But they also make up their own minds in the voting booth and don't want the church involved in partisan politics.

SOCIAL AND POLITICAL ISSUES

What do Core Catholics think about some of the major social and political issues of the day? The Notre Dame study asked respondents to say whether they strongly favor, favor, oppose, or strongly oppose some specific proposals (Table 31). The most striking finding is the incredible level of support for a bilateral nuclear freeze—92 percent of those surveyed supported such a freeze. This survey was conducted in 1983, at the peak of publicity about the United States bishops' peace pastoral, and awareness of the pastoral seems responsible for the high level of support for a bilateral freeze. In national surveys, Catholics have been more supportive of a bilateral freeze than any other religious group. The Notre Dame study suggests that Core Catholics are even more supportive. At the same time, a full one-third of the Core Catholics sampled (35 percent) supported even a unilateral United States freeze on nuclear weapons development. This surprising figure suggests the depth of concern about the nuclear arms race among Core Catholics.

Table 31. **Core Catholic Opinion on Social and Political Issues**

ISSUE	STRONGLY FAVOR (%)	FAVOR (%)	OPPOSE (%)	STRONGLY OPPOSE (%)
Registration of all firearms	42	32	15	11
Death penalty for persons convicted of murder	22	43	27	7

ISSUE	STRONGLY FAVOR (%)	FAVOR (%)	OPPOSE (%)	STRONGLY OPPOSE (%)
The equal rights amendment (ERA)	21	48	22	9
Increased spending for national defense	8	41	36	15
A "freeze" on the development of nuclear weapons by our own government, regardless of what the Soviet Union does	11	24	44	21
A joint "freeze" on the development of nuclear weapons by both the United States and the Soviet Union	53	39	5	3
A boycott of those companies which sponsor television shows having morally objectionable content	22	50	23	6

Core Catholics are about evenly divided between those who favor higher defense spending and those who do not, but support is not enthusiastic—only 8 percent strongly favor increased defense spending.

Catholic concern for arms control goes beyond nuclear weapons and extends to personal firearms—three Core Catholics in four (74 percent) favor registration of all firearms. On this social issue, Core Catholics find themselves on the "liberal" end of the spectrum, but their strong support for the death penalty—65 percent—places them on the "conservative" end of the spectrum on that issue.

This is not the only time Catholics defy conventional political labels. For example, support for legal restrictions on abortion is considered "conservative" and is often linked with opposition to women's rights. Yet when it comes to the Equal Rights Amendment, Core Catholics are strong supporters—seven in ten (69 percent) favor the amendment.

Do these views reflect any influence by the United States bishops, who have taken positions on a number of political issues? Comparing these findings with comparable questions on national opinion surveys allows us to answer this question: on some issues, Core Catholics do seem influenced by their bishops, while on others they do not. For example, the extremely high support for a bilateral nuclear freeze clearly reflects the priority the bishops have placed on the arms control issues. Similarly, while the Notre Dame study did not ask any questions about specific antiabortion legislation, the Core Catholics in the study are considerably more antiabortion than Catholics who are not parish-connected. Particularly interesting is the fact that while a majority of Core Catholics reject the bishops' opposition to capital punishment, the one-third of Core Catholics who agreed with the bishops is almost twice as high as the number of those opposing capital punishment in national surveys. On the other hand, Core Catholics support the ERA even though the bishops, while officially neutral on the amendment, have emphasized caution because of their concern that ratifying the ERA would strengthen the legality of abortion. Core Catholics, then, seem willing to listen to what the bishops say about specific political issues, but—and by now this should be no surprise—they continue to make up their own minds about those issues.

CONCLUSIONS

Vatican II encouraged Catholics to become more involved ecumenically and socially. Ecumenism and social action are, understandably, not as entrenched in American parish life as activities such as religious education and social service which have a longer history. But parishes have made great strides in ecumenism and social action.

What is most impressive, however, is the discovery that parish activity lags considerably behind the views of the people—Core

Catholics are even more disposed toward ecumenism and social action than church leaders realize. The support for a structural approach to justice and peace is particularly surprising. All this means that there is great potential for an explosion of ecumenical cooperation and social action at the parish level in the coming decades.

NOTE

Material in this chapter is based on the parishioner survey and on-site reports.

11. Parish Life and Laity— Into the Future

The parish is the central structure through which Catholics experience, nurture, and act out their faith. It is a community of a particular people living in a particular society as part of an international church. Throughout American history, and particularly since Vatican II, American Catholics, American society, and the Roman Catholic Church have all changed substantially, dramatically, and sometimes suddenly. The Notre Dame Study of Catholic Parish Life provides a historic profile of the nature of the post-Vatican II American Catholic parish and offers a basis for anticipating future changes and needs.

The study confirms that the life and personality of each parish are shaped by its own unique history and environment, reflecting its place in the broader society. The most important fact about the relationship of the parish to society in the early days of the United States was that the parish served largely as a refuge for new, impoverished immigrants in a Protestant society which for the most part rejected them. But that aspect of American society no longer exists. Americans have elected a Catholic president. Both parties have nominated Catholic vice-presidential candidates. We have had a popular Catholic speaker of the House. Catholics make up the largest religious group in Congress, and Catholics have been elected to the Senate in places like Oklahoma and Alabama. Lee Iacocca, the son of Italian Catholic immigrants, has topped some lists of the most admired men in America. While anti-Catholicism has not disappeared, Catholics are firmly anchored in the American mainstream.

Other changes in American society filter down into parish life.

United States society in general has grown more diverse and more tolerant of diversity. The long-term trend has been toward greater equality and expansion of rights for members of minority groups and women. Participatory democracy has become more and more widespread. Americans are congenitally independent, and they want a say in the running of whatever institutions to which they belong—government, business, labor unions, churches. Always distrustful of political power, Americans have become even more skeptical of institutional power since the Watergate era. All of this has taken place against a backdrop of increased income and education and a massive suburbanization in which people from diverse backgrounds come together in new communities with fewer attachments than were found in ethnic urban enclaves.

As American society has changed, so have American Catholics. While new waves of Hispanic and Asian-American immigrants show that immigration is a continuing feature of American Catholicism, the sons and daughters of past immigrants have become affluent and educated, mirroring the general population. Their success and acceptance have given them a greater sense of security and confidence. They don't live or work in religious and ethnic ghettoes; they live and work with Americans from all backgrounds.

These changes in American society and American Catholics formed the context for the American reception of the Second Vatican Council with its emphasis on shared responsibility, lay ministry, and opening a window on the world. David Leege notes that "when the Church began to view itself as a People of God, it found an American Catholic lay populace with many of the advantages of education and with middle-class outlooks that made it ready to assume responsibility for the People of God." The result has been a historic shift in the role of the American Catholic parish: The parish is no longer a haven from the secular world and Protestant bigotry. It is a vehicle for both experiencing the faith and for motivating Catholics to relate to the broader community and to shape it according to Gospel values.

THE IMPACT OF VATICAN II

We can and will point to specific areas in which Vatican II changed the shape of American Catholic parish life. But the overriding importance of the Council is both less tangible and more important than any one specific change. The Second Vatican Council changed the way the Catholic church thinks about itself and the way its members think about their church. Vatican II, with its proclamation of the theology of the People of God, was in many ways a churchwide exercise in community organization, in the building of community. Just as community organizations create a sense of ownership of neighborhoods and institutions, Vatican II extended participation in church life and therefore increased the sense of ownership which Catholics feel about their church. This sense of ownership has led to increased lay participation in church activity and more widespread lay leadership.

The sense of ownership stirred by Vatican II led naturally to a greater acceptance of pluralism. The decision to allow the celebration of Mass in the vernacular symbolized the legitimacy of pluralism. Pluralism breeds more pluralism. So, for example, conservative and liberal Catholics, Charismatics, and those with a pre-Vatican II style of devotion, all coexist in the same parish.

The renewed sense of ownership of the church has also created a new understanding of religious education. For today's parish-connected Catholics, religious education is not simply a matter of passing a static faith on to their children. It is a matter of passing on the core of the faith to the young while continuing their own process of education in a growing, developing faith with continually new implications.

And just as neighborhood community organizations are formed to have an impact on forces affecting the wider society, Vatican II has empowered the church to play a more active and visible role in shaping the local, national, and world community. This is most visible in two areas—Catholic schools and parish justice and peace programs. Catholic schools are no longer a haven for poor Catholics; they are increasingly a ministry to the non-Catholic poor in the inner city. The rapid growth of parish justice and peace programs since the Council signifies that the acceptance of the need for structural reforms as well as direct services to the poor has taken root among Core Catholics.

Participation ranked at the top of reasons pastors and administrators cited for the presence of vitality in their parishes. This was expressed in several ways. In the 1,099 parishes surveyed, 20 percent of pastors and parish administrators cited high involvement by the laity, 19 percent cited the unique feeling of community in their particular parish, 15 percent cited the parish council, 14 percent cited the support of the people, and 13 percent cited the vision of parish leadership.

The best place to see the new church participation is in the liturgy itself. Today's Core Catholics join their parishes and take part in the liturgy out of choice, not duty. They do so because they get what they want—spirituality, community, an opportunity to serve. Their parishes provide a variety of worship styles, institutionalizing pluralism to satisfy the different liturgical tastes of their parishioners.

The Vatican II changes which increase participation in the liturgy are immensely popular with Core Catholics: of those surveyed only 4 percent object to congregational hymn singing, only 6 percent to lay readers, only 10 percent to Communion in the hand, and only 12 percent to the Sign of Peace. Even the most controversial change, the use of women eucharistic ministers, is objected to by less than one-fifth (18 percent) of Core Catholics.

In addition, David Leege and Mark Searle's analysis found that the parishes in which people are the least satisfied with their liturgies are the ones which do not reflect Vatican II reforms and that the parishes in which people are most satisfied with their liturgies are those which do reflect the post-Vatican II liturgy.

Almost all of the factors which seem to be associated with good liturgies—or at least liturgies in which people are most likely to take part with enthusiasm—reflect lay participation and ownership: good planning, rehearsal of hymns before Mass, a greeting by the priest to the congregation and a rapport which reflects a sense of community, homilies which address the people as a congregation, music appropriate to the Mass, and a social gathering after Mass.

Another expression of lay people's increased sense of ownership of the church is the degree to which they now lead it at the parish level. While the pastor is still the central parish figure, in two-thirds of the United States Catholic parishes we studied, he heads a pastoral team composed primarily of lay men and women. Eighty-three percent of those identified as parish leaders (apart from pastors) are lay people. In perhaps 10 percent of United States parishes, someone other than the pastor is functionally the most important leader. Thirty percent of American parishes employ lay persons specifically for pastoral ministry, and lay people account for fifty-seven percent of the top leadership on parish staff. Three-quarters of all parishes have parish councils.

The sense of participation and ownership sparked by Vatican II has led to an explosion of new programs and activities within the parish. In addition to traditional activities such as religious education for children; grade schools; care for the sick and aged; social services; and choirs, parishes now provide parish councils; liturgy planning groups; adult religious education; youth ministry; music and cultural activities; marriage and family development programs and programs for the separated and divorced; small groups for prayer, reflection, and Bible reading; ministry training programs; charismatic groups; evangelization and social action programs.

Those programs are clearly being utilized. The Notre Dame study found that 48 percent of Core Catholics take part in at least one parish activity outside of Mass, and about half of those take part in more than one. Thirty percent of those Core Catholics involved spend an average of five hours per month on parish activities, and 15 percent spend more than fifteen hours a month. The figures are even higher for parish volunteers.

Substantial percentages of Core Catholics want even more services and programs from their parishes. They want more religious education, particularly for adults; more evangelization; more help for the poor; more ecumenical involvement and more social action; more help with marital problems, drug and alcohol abuse, and financial difficulties.

Finally, the Vatican II engendered sense of lay ownership of the church is reflected in the growing reliance by Core Catholics on their own consciences instead of church teaching in deciding what is moral and what is best for the church. We emphasize again that the Core Catholics in our sample are not "traditionalists"; they insisted on making up their own minds. Two-thirds reject church teaching on birth control and divorce. A similar proportion approves of abortion in cases, such as rape and incest, which are rejected by the church. Only slightly smaller numbers would accept a married priesthood.

Church leaders may regret this independence. But they themselves have helped foster it, and it is not likely to disappear.

If the mark of the success of a policy is whether people want more of it, then Vatican II's "community organization" has been an overwhelming success in the United States. Core Catholics want more changes in the direction of those called for by the Council. In our study, 76 percent want the church to become more "people-oriented" and "less concerned about its organizational structures and rules"; 80 percent say the church should listen more to the voice of ordinary lay Catholics; 74 percent believe the church should not de-emphasize lay involvement in the liturgy.

Furthermore, Core Catholics expect more change in this direction. Sixteen percent told us they expect a great deal of change in the future, 65 percent expect some change, and only 19 percent expect no change. Most of the specific changes mentioned involved greater lay participation in parish life. The only other possible changes mentioned in any significant degree were expectations that a pastor would leave or that the parish would grow. There is no doubt that Core Catholics firmly believe that they share in the "ownership" of their church.

THE STATE OF THE PARISH

The Notre Dame study found a vast diversity among American parishes. But one conclusion seems warranted—despite some problem areas, the post-Vatican II Catholic parish in the United States is basically healthy. It plays a central role in the lives of its parishioners and continues to change to accommodate a changing people and a changing church.

One measure of vitality is the degree of satisfaction Core Catholics feel about their parish:

- Core Catholics attend their territorial parish because they want to, not because they feel obligated to do so.
- Eighty-five percent of Core Catholics say their parish meets their spiritual needs "completely" or "very well." This figure is extremely high and represents a significant degree of satisfaction.
- Fifty-six percent of Core Catholics say their parish meets their social needs "completely" or "very well." While understandably much lower than the percentage giving similar ratings to the parish for meeting their spiritual needs, this figure too is impressive. We expect Catholics to turn to their parish for spiritual needs—this is an area with little competition. But there is a considerable amount of competition for social life, and we would not expect Catholics to turn to the parish as their primary social focus. The fact that so many Core Catholics are involved in the social life of the parish indicates that they get involved by choice.
- Core Catholics are enthusiastic about the liturgical reforms brought about by Vatican II. Fewer than one in ten find the music, singing, readings, prayers, and ritual at Mass unsatisfactory.
- As noted in Chapter 4, we estimate that the parish provides a real sense of community for about half of Core Catholics. Church leaders would, of course, prefer this to be even higher. But this is still an astounding figure.

In assessing the health of the parish today, however, it is important to distinguish the circumstances of urban, suburban, small town, and rural parishes. All have their own strengths and weaknesses.

The Notre Dame study reveals that small town and rural parishes are one of the most neglected elements within the church. Many of these parishes have a strong sense of community, but that sense seems more related to a homogeneous local community than to a sense of church. Rural parishes are less likely than others to have implemented Vatican II liturgical reforms and, largely because of their small size, less likely to have more than rudimentary parish programs. Perhaps a quarter to a third of these are assigned pastors who do not agree with the "community-building" theology of Vatican II. It is the small rural parishes which will first feel the impact of the priest shortage. For example, some of the rural parishes studied in depth were already served by a circuit rider or thought they would not be assigned a new resident pastor when their current pastor retired. The inherited sense of community found in rural parishes may be masking serious problems. Those in which pastors have not prepared the people for lay leadership could wither and die.

Urban parishes also reflect a strong sense of community, often stemming from relative ethnic neighborhood homogeneity. These parishes are usually larger than average and have more programs and services as well as a post-Vatican II liturgy. The major challenges to urban parishes seem to come from outside the church structure—from changing neighborhoods. Often, as in the past, this means racial change as blacks and Hispanics move into previously white neighborhoods. But, more and more often, urban parishes are in neighborhoods which are changing in a different way—"gentrification"—as young professionals move into and take over older neighborhoods.

But, by far, the most fascinating parishes today are in the suburbs. They are fascinating in large part because they are still relatively new, without the deep roots of many urban and rural parishes. They represent a new form of community. We've already noted that suburban Catholics in the study were the least attached to their parishes, with fewer close friends within their borders and fewer contacts with fellow parishioners. They are slightly less likely than Catholics in other types of parishes to say their parish meets their spiritual needs and substantially less likely to say it meets their social needs.

These findings tend to confirm the conventional wisdom within the church that something is somehow suspect about suburban parishes. There is a tendency in some church circles to view suburban parishes as selfish and resistant to community. But we believe this is a mistake. It is misleading to compare parishes in relatively new suburbs, a heterogeneous community, with urban and rural parishes, which have a long history and homogeneous community. Instead of comparing suburban parishes to mythical, ideal urban and rural parishes, we should view them as the pioneering ventures that they are. In that context, the amount of community which exists in these parishes—community which has in a sense been built out of nothing—is significant. Consider these findings:

- Suburban parishes, largely because of their size, tend to have more programs and services than are found in other types of parishes.
- Suburban parishes are more likely to have marriage and family programs and ministry to the separated and divorced, apparently reflecting sensitivity to the needs of their parishioners.
- Suburban parishes are more likely than the average to have adult religious education programs, indicating a seriousness about the faith.
- Far from being "selfish," suburban parishes are more likely than the average to have social service programs (65 percent) and social action programs (27 percent), indicating both a concern with traditional charity and a growing acceptance of the Council's emphasis on a structural response to social injustice.
- Suburban parishes are at the forefront of those parishes implementing Vatican II reforms and are more likely than either urban or rural parishes to express a strong sense of community within the liturgy itself.

• Despite the advantage of history and homogeneity possessed by urban and rural parishes, parishioners in suburban parishes still attribute a slightly stronger sense of community to their parish.

All of this suggests that suburban parishes have been given a "bad rap" by some in the church. The suburban parish is at the cutting edge of change within the church.

PROBLEMS AND OPPORTUNITIES

For the first time in the history of the Catholic church in the United States, the percentage of priests to laity is shrinking, while Catholic theology is encouraging the expansion of lay ministries. The growth of lay leadership is a matter of both choice and necessity: choice, because of the Vatican II theology of the People of God, and necessity, because of the combination of fewer priests and increased demand for services and ministry.

An expanded lay ministry can help American Catholic parishes cope with a problem which has become more acute since Vatican II—pastor separation anxiety. Before the Council, pastors generally left their posts by dying or retiring at a ripe old age. But with the limited tenure of pastors introduced after the Council, more and more parishes must face the challenge of the transition which comes when a pastor leaves—and they must face it more and more often. If lay involvement in leadership is institutionalized within a parish, however, the transition from one pastor to another can be made far easier—for both the new pastor and the congregation.

Given the newness of shared responsibility in the parish, it is not surprising that there have been some celebrated instances in which parishes have been torn apart by conflicts over leadership and lay involvement. But, given the magnitude of the changes in the parish sparked by Vatican II, the real news is how few parishes have been crippled by conflict; only a handful of the nation's nineteen thousand Catholic parishes have gone through such turmoil.

Three-quarters of the thirty-six parishes observed in depth in the Notre Dame study reported some degree of conflict, suggesting that conflict is widespread within American parishes. But the vast majority of the churches reporting conflict also reported that those conflicts were resolved. Conflict in parishes, as in personal relationships, is natural, and American Catholic parishes are learning this. Tension is a sign of life. Parishes with little or no conflict showed some signs of dying.

The Notre Dame study surfaced some potential areas of conflict which bear watching. For example, the study found that a disproportionate number of those with a preconciliar orientation (conservatives) and a postconciliar orientation (progressives) become involved in parish government, setting the stage for division. Similarly, the study found discontent among women in parish leadership positions because, while they outnumber men in leadership roles, they are often frozen out of top decision-making posts. There is also likely to be a continued tension between a church which is still hierarchical in nature and its people who want a more democratic structure.

The most fascinating source of conflict found by the Notre Dame study is a major perception gap—actually, a series of perception gaps—involving almost all possible combinations of pastors, staff, volunteers, and parishioners. For example:

- Asked to surmise the way their pastor would respond to thirteen questions about church teachings and policies, 37 percent of parishioners misperceived their pastor's views. Asked to predict their parishioners' responses to the same questions, 28 percent of the pastors misperceived their parishioners' views.
- Parishioners seem to be unaware of a "silent opposition" among pastors to some church teachings. For example, in one parish in six, parishioners did not realize that their pastor believes the church's position on abortion is too rigid. Fourteen of thirty-six pastors were opposed to the church's teaching on contraception, but parishioners in only one of the fourteen parishes knew this. Sixteen pastors supported ordaining married men and eleven supported ordaining women. But parishioners in only

two parishes knew their pastor supported ordaining married men. And there was no parish in which a majority of parishioners realized their pastor supported women's ordination.

- Parishioners underestimated their pastor's commitment to lay participation in the liturgy and a "people-centered" church.
- Pastors underestimated their parishioners' commitment to intercommunion with other Christians, while parishioners' overestimated their pastor's commitment.
- Pastors believe they are sharing power, but that perception is not always shared by those around them. Almost all of the pastors in the 36-parish sample said the parish council did "planning," while one-third of staff members and almost half of volunteer leaders believe the council does not plan.
- The pastor believes he plays a smaller role in running parish programs than staff and volunteers believe he plays, particularly in the liturgy and social action programs.
- While 90 percent of volunteer leaders felt they had at least some influence on the pastor, council, and staff, about 40 percent said they wanted more influence.
- Pastors are about twice as likely as staff and volunteers to say conflict originates within the parish council and that it pits the council against the pastor.
- Pastors in three-fourths of the parishes reporting conflict are confident that conflict is resolved without one side or the other "winning," but other leaders are more likely to believe that the pastor "wins" such conflicts.
- Lay leaders often judge parish decision-making processes by a "democratic model," while pastors almost always use either a "consultative model" or an "authoritarian model."

It would be unrealistic to expect pastors and parishioners or parish leaders to be one-hundred percent accurate in their perceptions of others' beliefs or in their characterizations of parish activity. But the sizeable perception gaps which do exist make it clear that parish leaders and parishioners need to spend some more time talking frankly to one another.

The Notre Dame study spotlights some other areas of concern that demand attention in the near future:

- Greater attention must be given to the needs of Hispanic Catholics who are devotionally pious, but often not well integrated into parish leadership structures. The economic circumstances of many Hispanics, the continual flow of new immigrants, the large number of Hispanic children, and the lack of knowledge about current church teaching and life all pose substantial pastoral challenges.
- There is considerable confusion in American parishes about communal penance. About half of Core Catholics are not aware that the church sanctions use of a communal penance service in conjunction with private Confession.
- There are signs that as lay men and women become more active in parish leadership, some cliques, what might be called a form of lay clericalism, are emerging, putting an artificial distance between parish leadership and parishioners.

GROWTH POTENTIAL

We have several times noted the explosion of parish services and programs since Vatican II. That explosion seems likely to continue as Core Catholics demand more from their parishes and as parishes expand existing ministries. Several areas are most likely to expand:

Leadership Training. Leadership training is already fairly widespread, and parish staff and volunteers are serious about their work, reading books and articles and attending workshops to hone their skills. Continued training is needed for two major reasons: to keep up with the growing demand for parish leaders and to improve the quality of parish leadership. The Notre Dame study has shown that occupying a key position does not by itself make a person a leader.

Marriage Counseling and Ministry to Separated, Divorced, and Remarried Catholics. This is an area where supply falls far behind demand. For example, 78 percent of Core Catholics say they would turn to the parish for premarital counseling, and 60 percent say they would turn to the parish for help with severe marital problems if it were available. But only 48 percent of parishes offer marriage and family development programs. The gap is even more acute when it comes to divorce—25 percent of Catholics who have married have been divorced, but only 20 percent of Catholic parishes have a program for divorced Catholics. This is of particular concern because there is a major gap between pastors and parishioners in attitudes toward divorce. Pastors greatly overestimate their parishioners' commitment to present church teaching on divorce, and parishioners greatly overestimate their pastors' support for it.

Drug and Alcohol Counseling. Fifty percent of Core Catholics say they would turn to the parish for help with drug and alcohol abuse if they needed it and it was available, while only 13 percent said their parish had such help now. Prevention of drug and alcohol abuse ranked at the top of possible areas for expanded parish activity—67 percent of Core Catholics said they wanted their parish to be more involved in this area, while only 13 percent said they wanted it to be less involved.

Financial Problems and Unemployment. About one-fourth of Core Catholics said they would turn to the parish for help with severe financial problems or if they were unemployed, but less than 10 percent said such help was available now. The figures on Catholic affluence sometimes obscure the fact that many Catholics are still poor and many middle-class Catholics are still threatened by recession, plant closings, and other economic disruptions. Dealing with these problems is not yet a parish priority.

Adult Religious Education. A surprising 63 percent of American Catholic parishes already have adult religious education programs, indicating a remarkably positive response since Vatican II. But the demand still exceeds the supply: 85 percent of Core Catholics say they would turn to the parish for religious education for themselves if it were available. This demand is likely to be fueled by follow-up activities to the United States bishops' 1983 pastoral letter on peace and their 1986 pastoral letter on the economy. Adult religious education is a major growth area for the years ahead.

Ecumenism. Thirty-eight percent of Core Catholics want ecumenical cooperation to be a higher priority for their parish, while only 15 percent want it to be a lower priority; seventy percent support intercommunion with other Christian churches. Ecumenical activity can solidify a parish's ties to its neighboring community. Core Catholics are happy with the ecumenical and interfaith cooperation spurred by the Council and they want more such activity on a day-to-day basis.

Social Service. Sixty percent of Core Catholics say they would turn to the parish for an opportunity to serve others, but only 48 percent say they can do so now, and only 52 percent of parishes have social service programs. Helping the poor within the parish is a high priority for Core Catholics, and serving as a focal point for charitable activity ranks only behind building a faith community as a description of what the parish should be. Social service is a well-established parish function with broad support which could be easily expanded.

Justice and Peace Programs. The growing opportunity for a justice and peace emphasis and parishioners' acceptance of the necessity for structural change is one of the most significant findings of the Notre Dame study. While parish social action programs were rare before Vatican II, by the time of the study 20 percent of parishes—including 27 percent in the suburbs and 29 percent in urban areas—now have such programs. Thirty-seven percent of Core Catholics want more parish activity to "change unjust socio-economic conditions," while 21 percent want less. Fifty-two percent say they feel close to God while working for justice and peace, and, while this ranks behind activities such as receiving Communion and praying, it ranks ahead of Bible reading and "obeying Church rules." The growing acceptance of the social action approach plus the incentive of the follow-up to the bishops' peace and economic pastorals make justice and peace programs another growth industry within the parish.

THE NOTRE DAME STUDY

Neither of the present authors was involved in the inception of the Notre Dame Study of Catholic Parish Life, so we feel that it is not self-serving to emphasize the landmark nature of this study. In writing this book, time and time again we faced the same frustration—we had fascinating information from the study, but nothing with which to compare it. No study is flawless, but the major flaw about the Notre Dame study is that nothing so systematic and comprehensive across such a large number of parishes nationwide was done before. It would now be invaluable to have similar data available from a parish life survey made, for instance, in the late 1950s, just before Vatican II.

Aside from specific findings, the Notre Dame study offers two dimensions which could have a lasting impact. The first is the detailed survey of Core Catholics or parish-connected Catholics. This unprecedented survey provides a wealth of information about a unique group of American Catholics—those actually engaged in parish life, the backbone and heartbeat of the United States church.

The second major contribution of the Notre Dame study lies in its basic conception—an interdisciplinary look inside the parish. The Catholic church has lagged behind other denominations in its use of social science research and, like other denominations, has a tendency to take a fragmented approach to church activity: church leaders concentrate on liturgy or social action or parochial schools or religious education or theology. But it is misleading to focus on any particular area without an awareness of the integrated life of the entire parish—and of the national and local history which have shaped it.

The Notre Dame study shows that, to an increasing degree since Vatican II, many pastors and church officials, religious, and lay leaders conceive of and deal with the parish as an integrated, life-giving community. With its own history, self-awareness, and future, the living parish of Vatican II animates lay participation and communal purposes throughout the People of God and similarly enlivens secular society.

Scholarly and journalistic writers on religious issues usually focus, for understandable reasons, on the highest echelons of the church, especially on activities of the American bishops, famous theologians, and the Vatican—as though these encompass the living church. The lowly parish is easily ignored. In the 1970s, some postulated its decline, even its death.

This study now affirms this central reality of the contemporary Catholic church USA: It is mainly in and through the local congregation, the parish, that the church lives on, because that is *where the people are*. And "where two or three are gathered together in my name, there am I in the midst of them."

Acknowledgments

The idea for the Notre Dame Study of Catholic Parish Life originated after the 1980 publication of the United States bishops' statement, *The Parish: A People, A Mission, A Structure*. Father Philip Murnion, who directed the bishops' parish project, and Msgr. John Egan, director of Notre Dame's Institute for Pastoral and Social Ministry, worked together to conceive the study. Father Hesburgh strongly supported a request to Lilly Endowment, Inc., which made a grant to fund the study.

Murnion supervised Phase I, 1981–83, which obtained basic data from 1,099 parishes. In consultation with David Leege, director of the Notre Dame Center for the Study of Contemporary Society, he also prepared the far-reaching plan for Phase II, 1982–86, which did in-depth research into 36 parishes. Leege was named director for the scientific team which produced and analyzed ethnographic reports of on-site visits, observations of weekend Masses, leader interviews, comprehensive histories of parishes in the six United States regions, and questionnaires completed by 2,667 parishioners, 212 volunteer leaders, 89 paid staff, and 35 pastors. In 1984, as the study team began to address data now pouring in, Joseph Gremillion, Egan's successor since July 1983 at the Institute for Ministry, became director of Phase III: interpreting, communicating, and applying the study's findings. Gremillion was succeeded in August 1986 by Father Robert Pelton, C.S.C., new director of the Institute for Pastoral and Social Ministry.

At the initiative of Frank Butler, president of FADICA (Foundations and Donors Interested in Catholic Activities), that body sponsored a conference to introduce the study's early findings in Chicago in May 1985. This session was reported in a 100-page booklet, *The Parish in Transition*, published by the United States

Catholic Conference and edited by David Byers. It was, in turn, a resource in the preparation of this book.

Three member organizations of FADICA have cooperatively provided funding for publishing the study reports cited above, and we want to extend our thanks to FADICA and its member bodies.

It was FADICA president Butler who suggested to Jim Castelli, a journalist familiar with both Catholic affairs and social science writing, that he contact Gremillion about writing a popular-style book on the study's findings.

The result, *The Emerging Parish,* is based on literally thousands of pages of research generated by the Notre Dame study. The principal source was a series of scholarly reports issued by the university since December 1984. Gremillion and Leege are coeditors of the report series. Leege, however, has been the principal writer, assisted by a dozen collaborators and specialized consultants. Leege was responsible for identifying and extracting from the data bank of 6.8 million computer bytes those elements needed in printout form. He has also served as the main interpreter of the data. Leege served as head of the scientific team for the indepth research phase, along with Dr. Mark Searle for liturgy, Dr. Jay Dolan for history, and Dr. Michael Welch for social and organizational studies.

The report numbers, titles, and authors follow:

1. *The U.S. Parish Twenty Years After Vatican II: An Introduction to the Study* (December 1984), Leege and Gremillion.
2. *A Profile of American Catholic Parishes and Parishioners: 1820s to the 1980s* (February 1985), Dolan and Leege.
3. *Participation in Catholic Parish Life: Religious Rites and Parish Activities in the 1980s* (April 1985), Leege and Thomas Trozzolo.
4. *Religious Values and Parish Participation: The Paradox of Individual Needs in a Communitarian Church* (June 1985), Leege and Trozzolo. Consultants were Professor Dean Hoge, Department of Sociology, Catholic University of America; and Father Philip Murnion.

5. *The Celebration of Liturgy in the Parishes* (August 1985), Mark Searle and Leege. Consultants were Father Robert Schmitz of the Cincinnati Archdiocesan Office of Planning and Research; and Sister Eleanor Bernstein of the Center for Pastoral Liturgy, University of Notre Dame.

6. *Of Piety and Planning: Liturgy, the Parishioners and the Professionals* (December 1985), Searle and Leege. Consultants were Schmitz; Bernstein; and Sister Kathleen Hughes of the Catholic Theological Union, University of Chicago.

7. *The People, Their Pastors and the Church: Viewpoints on Church Policies and Positions* (March 1986), Leege and Gremillion. Consultants were Sister Agnes Cunningham of Saint Mary of the Lake University, Mundelein Seminary; Father Timothy O'Connell of the Institute for Pastoral Studies, Loyola University of Chicago; and Hoge.

8. *Parish Organizations: People's Needs, Parish Services and Leadership* (July 1986), Leege. Consultants were Professor Richard Schoenherr of the Department of Sociology, University of Wisconsin-Madison; Hoge; and Murnion.

9. *Parish Life Among the Leaders* (December 1986), Leege. Consultants were Sister Donna Watzke, O.P., former director of pastoral planning for the Diocese of Fort Wayne–South Bend and currently a psychiatric social worker at Saint Vincent's Stress Center, Indianapolis, IN; and Kathryn O'Hara, an elementary school teacher in South Bend, IN, who has served as chair of a diocesan pastoral council and in several parish leadership positions; and Murnion.

10. *Parish and Community* (March 1987), Leege. Consultants were Hoge and Watzke.

These reports, singly or as a series, may be ordered from the Notre Dame Parish Study, 1201 Memorial Library, Notre Dame, IN 46556. As many as five more reports are projected by the end of 1988.

The other principal published product of the study used here was *The American Catholic Parish: A History From 1850 to the Present,* edited by Jay Dolan (Paulist Press, 1987). Dolan headed the historical team of six authors, each of whom researched and wrote up the parish history of a region. The authors and their respective regions were Dr. Jeffrey Burns (Pacific coast), Dr. Joseph Casino (northeast), Carol Jensen (inter-mountain), Rev. Michael McNally (south Atlantic), Dr. Charles Nolan (south central), and Dr. Stephen Shaw (the Midwest). Their 1,300-page manuscript is sampled in Chapter 2. We express gratitude to Dr. Dolan and Paulist Press for allowing use here of their copyrighted material.

Some material for this book came from data printouts not cited in the report series. Also used were the reports of two on-site visitors to each of the thirty-six parishes studied in depth. Sixteen liturgists and social scientists made these reports based on an average of 3 ½ days, always over a weekend, at the parishes: Kimberly Baldt-Numan, Michael Ball, Edith Batz, Dr. Elizabeth Briody, Barbara Budde, Rev. David Clark, Thomas Dowdy, Dr. Roger Finke, Sister Jennifer Glen, Rev. Everett Hemann, Dr. Donald LeMagdeleine, Sister Camille Martinez, Michael Meacham, Rev. Thomas Ryan, Rev. Thomas Splain, and Sister Sharon Stola.

In Chapter 5, "The Hispanic Community, we made liberal use of *The Hispanic Catholic in the United States,* by Roberto Gonzalez and Michael Lavelle (1985). To them and their publisher, the Northeast Catholic Pastoral Center for Hispanics in New York, we also extend thanks for permission to use their material. We also used an unpublished report on Hispanic parishes made for the Notre Dame study from its own data bank by Dr. C. Lincoln Johnson, director of the university's Social Science Training and Research Laboratory, with the assistance of Thomas Trozzolo.

The role of officers and staff at Notre Dame is also gladly recognized, especially that of JoAnn Gabrich and Margaret Boggs, administrative secretaries at the Center for the Study of Contemporary Society and the Institute for Pastoral and Social Ministry, and D'Arcy Chisolm, the institute's assistant director who tended especially to accounting and printing needs. We also thank the computer inputters and retrievers, Thomas Trozzolo and Edwin

Hernandez, together with the score of data encoders, under the direction of Elizabeth Ann Bromley (for surveys) and Patricia Ann Leege (for liturgies).

We should also note that members of the Notre Dame study research team are now at work on further interpretation of the information gathered by the study. David Leege and Michael Welch are analyzing "religious convictions and political attitudes" among parishioners. Mark Searle is doing more in-depth research into liturgical symbols, stimulated in part by insights offered by the liturgical dimension of the study, which he directed. His writings are already appearing in appropriate journals.

Our book obviously owes a great deal to those who designed and implemented the Notre Dame study and interpreted its results, and we want to extend our gratitude to them. They have provided much of the book's data and some of its interpretation. In particular, we extend special acknowledgment to Dr. Leege, coeditor and principal writer for the reports listed above, for his permission to use major portions of their comment with only occasional attribution or direct quotes. We thank him, too, for his help in planning our book, for reading most of the chapters, and for offering his advice. We also express gratitude to Professors Dolan and Searle for similar help with the chapters on parish history, liturgy, and devotion.

However, all decisions about the selection and presentation of data, most of the interpretation, and all projections into the future are the sole responsibility of the authors, Castelli and Gremillion.

Finally, we wish to recognize our serious responsibility to the University of Notre Dame which has entrusted us with this presentation of a pioneering study of a topic so vast, significant, and timely: the maturing People of God in their local Catholic communities, since Vatican II, in the Christian church of North America.

Discussion Outline

One goal of the Notre Dame Study of Catholic Parish Life is to encourage awareness of parish life at all levels in the church. *The Emerging Parish* is particularly useful for members of parish councils, parish staff, and small groups of concerned parishioners in applying the Notre Dame study's findings to their own situation. The following questions are designed to make this book more useful in stimulating reflection or small group discussion about parish life.

CHAPTER 2

1. The Notre Dame study divided the Catholic church in the United States into six regions: northeast, south Atlantic, south central, Midwest, intermountain, and Pacific coast. To which region does your parish belong? How has the history of your region affected the history of your parish?

2. Is there a written history of your parish? Are parishioners aware of major events and personalities in the parish's history? How is your parish's identity shaped by its history? Are parish documents, bulletins, jubilee publications, photographs, etc. being preserved? Who is your parish historian?

3. Anti-Catholicism marked the early days of the Catholic church in the United States, but there were also many examples of interfaith cooperation. What has been the relationship of Catholics and non-Catholics in your community?

4. Lay persons played prominent roles in the founding and early development of many parishes, as did bishops, neighboring pastors, and religious missionaries. What has been the history of interaction among laity, clergy, and religious in the leadership and growth of your parish?

5. A historical overview points out the various forces which have affected the life of American parishes. What social, economic, political, and other forces have affected your parish in the past? And which are shaping life in your parish today?

6. The long-range trend shows an increasing number of Catholics per priest. What impact, if any, has the declining number of priests had on your parish? What is likely to be the impact in the future?

CHAPTER 3

1. How do the demographics in your parish compare to the overall profile of Core Catholics, or parish-connected Catholics?

2. This chapter reports the views of Core Catholics on major church policies and teachings. How do you suppose the majority of members of your parish feel about these issues?

3. Sometimes there is a great deal of consensus on these issues within a parish and sometimes there is not. Do you think there is much consensus within your parish? What about neighboring parishes?

4. The Notre Dame study found that pastors and parishioners think they know each other's beliefs, but often do not. Is there a "perception gap" between pastor and parishioners in your parish? On what issues?

5. The chapter reports the views of Core Catholics on when a person is or is not a "true" Catholic. What does this term mean to you, and how do you think members of your parish would respond?

CHAPTER 4

1. How would you describe the purpose of your parish?

2. How satisfied are parishioners with your parish? How well does it meet their spiritual needs? their social needs?

3. This chapter lists the wide variety of parish programs found

today. Which programs does your parish have? Should it have others? Why?

4. This chapter divides parishes into four types: simple, moderately complex, complex, and very complex. Which type is your parish? In what ways have various leaders helped it develop as a simple or complex parish, or perhaps limited its development?

5. What programs and activities should have top priority for your parish?

6. The Notre Dame study found that forty-eight percent of Core Catholics participated in church activities in addition to Mass. What percentage would you say participate in your parish? How could this figure be increased?

7. Which programs and activities give your parish vitality? Why?

CHAPTER 5

1. This chapter reports large increases in the number of Hispanic Catholics since the 1950s. Has their number increased in your region? your diocese? your neighborhood and parish? Estimate the number and percentage in each.

2. Is any weekend liturgy in your parish conducted in Spanish? If not, is this needed?

3. If there are Hispanics in your parish, have the pastor and staff, lay leadership, and people as a whole welcomed them as fellow Catholics? Have they entered into its activities? If so, which activities? If not, why not?

4. If *you* are a Hispanic Catholic who arrived in the parish in recent years, describe your own experience. If your parish is predominantly Hispanic, how are your relations with Catholics of other ethnic backgrounds?

5. Do Hispanics serve on the committees of your deanery or vicariate or diocese? Have Hispanics become active in the civic community and political life of your area?

6. Is there any tension between Hispanic Catholics and other religio-ethnic groups in your area? How many Hispanics are not

Catholics? Are there efforts by other churches to bring Catholic Hispanics into their congregations?

CHAPTER 6

1. The Notre Dame study notes that simply occupying a leadership position does not necessarily make a person a leader. Who are the real leaders in your parish? What makes them leaders? How many are lay men and women?

2. Does your parish have a leadership training program?

3. How are key decisions made in your parish? Does your parish have a parish council? Does it help make decisions? How do parishioners make their views known to parish leadership?

4. Is there a major on-going conflict in your parish? How are conflicts resolved?

5. How does your parish relate to the diocese? How do diocesan policies affect the parish?

6. Is your pastor nearing retirement or the end of a fixed tenure? How is your parish preparing for an eventual transition?

7. How well do lay leaders relate to others in the parish. Is there a lay leadership "clique"?

CHAPTER 7

1. The Notre Dame study found that in many parishes, a different style of liturgy is used at different Masses to meet a diversity in parish taste. Does your parish offer a variety of liturgical styles?

2. In many parishes, the Saturday evening Mass is not as well planned or celebrated as Sunday Masses. What is the Saturday evening Mass like in your parish?

3. This chapter describes a number of liturgical changes made by Vatican II. Are these reforms found in your parish? Are they popular with the people? Has your parish had sufficient education about the liturgical reforms?

4. The conclusion of this chapter lists a number of factors

which seem to be associated with successful liturgies. Which of these factors are present in your parish?

CHAPTER 8

1. What forms of public devotion are offered in your parish? Do any include public processions or fiestas outside the church building? on the street?

2. Do small groups gather for special devotions or prayer together? Are they encouraged, discouraged, or just ignored?

3. The Notre Dame study found that many parishes have their own "prayer culture" reflecting ethnic or other traditions. Does your parish have such a culture? What is its history? How long do you think that tradition will continue? Should it be encouraged?

4. What private or family devotions were practiced by your parents? Do you continue them? During the weekend Mass, do some parishioners say the Rosary or pray on their own? What percentage do this?

5. The Notre Dame study found a great deal of confusion about communal penance. Does your parish use communal penance rites involving private Confession? If so, what percentage go alone to a priest for Confession? Have the number of private Confessions lessened since Vatican II? If so, why? Have the hours of Saturday Confession increased or decreased?

CHAPTER 9

1. The Notre Dame study found that, since Vatican II, religious education has become a "womb-to-tomb" concern. What forms of religious education does your parish offer? A parish grade school? Religious education for elementary school students? for high school students? for adults?

2. If your parish has a grade school, how well regarded is it in your parish and community? What contribution does it make to overall parish life?

3. How well regarded is religious education (CCD) for children and youth? What contribution does it make to overall parish life?

4. What forms of adult education does your parish offer? When did it begin? How many parishioners participate? What is the age and gender breakdown of those who participate? Does the diocese promote adult education programs within or among parishes?

5. What relationship does your parish have to the public schools in your area? What percentage of your elementary and secondary school children attend Catholic schools? public schools?

6. Do adults from your parish seek religious education elsewhere, for example, in neighborhood Bible study groups, at local retreat centers or colleges, at non-Catholic churches?

CHAPTER 10

1. Vatican II greatly encouraged friendly relations with Protestants, Jews, and members of other faiths. How many other Christian churches can you name in your neighborhood or community? Synagogues? Mosques? Others?

2. Is your parish involved with any of these in interfaith or ecumenical activities? What kind? Are you personally involved?

3. Does your parish have a program for evangelization of the "unchurched" or for inviting nonpracticing Catholics back into active church life?

4. What opportunities does your parish offer for charitable and social service activities? Do many people participate?

5. Recently, the United States Catholic bishops have issued pastoral letters on peace and nuclear warfare and on the economy. Have they affected your parish programs? Does your parish teach about these letters?

6. Does your parish have a permanent program for social action to promote justice, peace, and human rights?

7. Does your parish have an on-going relationship with less well off parishes which includes financial assistance? (Or with "better-off" parishes from which help is received?)

8. What contribution do social service and social action pro-

grams make to the overall life of the parish? What effect do they have on the neighborhood and civic community?

9. This chapter lists several possible social service and social action priorities. Which should be priorities for your parish?

CHAPTER 11

1. This chapter talks about the growth of community within American parishes. How would you assess the level of community in your parish, and what can be done to improve it?

2. This chapter offers brief assessments of the state of urban, suburban, and rural parishes in the United States. Which type of parish is yours, and how does it compare to these assessments?

3. This chapter lists a number of areas of "growth potential" for American parishes. Is your parish likely to grow in any of these areas?

4. What will the future of your parish be like? What changes are likely and what factors are likely to shape the parish in the future? Are you preparing lay leaders and the parish as a whole for the 1990s and beyond?